NO BACK DOORS

The Charles Graham Story

By
Charles Graham

With
Darrel Campbell

Charles Graham Ministry

NO BACK DOORS

The Charles Graham Story

by

Charles Graham

With

Darrel Campbell

Published by Charles Graham Ministry, Inc.

Copyright © Charles Graham, 2019

All rights reserved. Written permission must be secured from the publisher to use or reproduce any part of this book, except for brief quotations in critical reviews of articles.

ISBN-13: 978-0578420943

Scripture quotations from The Authorized (King James) Version. Rights in the Authorized Version in the United Kingdom are vested in the Crown. Reproduced by permission of the Crown's patentee, Cambridge University Press Scripture taken from the Modern English Version. Copyright © 2014 by Military Bible Association. Used by Permission. All rights reserved.

Cover design by Darin Bell
Photography by Debbie McGee Gilbert

Printed in the United States of America

PUBLISHER'S NOTE:

While the author has made every effort to provide accurate telephone numbers, Internet addresses and other contact information at the time of publication, neither the publisher nor the author assumes any responsibility for errors, or for changes that occur after publication.

Charles Graham

Charles Graham Ministry

Dermott, AR 71638

Contact Charles Graham at:

charlesgrahamministry.com

DEDICATION

To my mother and father, Ollie and Willie Graham. Thank you for all the life lessons. And, to my twelve brothers and sisters: Dwight, Curtis, Willie (Angela), Stanley, Joyce (Jerry), Wanda (John), George, Fred (Shawn), Neddie, James (Marilyn), Grace (Kelvin), Jerry (Vanecia), nieces, nephews, and all of their families who remind me each day of just how blessed one man can be.

SPECIAL THANKS

My first thank you has to go to my Lord and Savior, Jesus Christ who loved me, saved me and inspired the journey that is shared in this book. I would like to say a special *thank you* to the many people around the world who helped make this book a reality. Thank you to the faithful supporters of Charles Graham Ministry. Because of your encouragement, this book was possible. Thank you Beth Berry, Doug Campbell, Shawna Teigen, Cindy Smith, and Mark Ehrich for your attention to detail as you edited this book.

TABLE OF CONTENTS

INTRODUCTION
PROLOGUE

CHAPTERS:

INTRODUCTION

In the pages ahead I'm very open about how I came to grips with the life and journey that God so graciously gave me. More than anything I want the reader to know that by choice, I packed up my life and moved back to live in the geographical location of my childhood hurts, pain, and confusion. It wasn't a nostalgic whim, but a mandate from God. In the pages of this book, I have attempted to convey my heart as I share with you the truth of my past. In no way did I attempt to shame or hurt the persons who impacted my life in a negative way, but I celebrate each life, each relationship as a building block of the amazing life that God has allowed me to live. It would bless me to know that readers might take a moment to think and examine their life after reading a book about mine. I want you to be inspired to live beyond your past hurts and disappointments. My prayer is that you will understand that the conditions you were born into do not define who you are, or what you may become. A fulfilling life begins with love and forgiveness that only God can teach you. These are the keys to a successful life.

PROLOGUE

I was nervous. All I could do was pray that I could make it through my first voice lesson without completely embarrassing myself. My family and friends understood that I was not your typical kid from Southeast Arkansas. Oh, sure, I was a tall and healthy African-American, but every time I was asked to join an athletic team or work as a farmer or laborer in the fields, it was like asking me to speak in another language. Deep in my heart, I knew that my God-given purpose in life was far from any athletic team or cotton field. I was certain that God wanted me to use my days on planet Earth singing ... for Him.

Nineteen years of age seemed old at the time of my first voice lesson, but due to my circumstances, it was the age I would begin my professional journey into music. Saying that I was unprepared for my first encounter with a voice teacher would be a severe understatement.

Music had always been a huge part of my daily life, but I was only familiar with the religious hymns, the music the congregation of my little country church had taught me, and the country music and Motown I could find on my little transistor radio. The one song I had memorized was, *He Touched Me*. I had heard it many times in churches. That's the song my university voice teacher would hear from me that fateful afternoon.

I was living far from home for the first time, and I had no family or close friends to lean on. People had always told me that I had a "large" singing voice and that I needed to let it be heard. It was the only way I knew to sing—big and strong. I cleared my throat as I stood in front of my voice instructor.

"Relax. Sing when you're ready, Charles," she said with an encouraging smile.

If she could only hear the prayers in my head at that moment—they went something like: *Please, God, let me perform well. I've traveled so far to start a journey toward what you want me to be. My family back in Dermott, Arkansas and the people of my church and community are counting on me to succeed. I made it out of my small town, and people are cheering me on.* I took a deep breath and began.

"Shackled by a heavy burden …" I began to sing at the top of my voice.

Like most inexperienced young singers, I'm sure I was watching my every move and making internal assessments of my voice. In other words, I was listening to myself, and to me, I sounded quite good! Best of all, I was certain that I had just made a very good impression.

As I found myself in front of the first professional voice coach of my life, I was sure that God had blessed me with a decent enough voice. He had also blessed me with His goodness and His mercy in my life, so singing songs that honored him was deeply rooted in who I was as a person.

My voice filled the room with the mighty phrases of the well-known song. The experience was surreal and exciting. I thought my voice sounded better than ever. I was exactly where I was meant to be, and I knew I was doing what I was supposed to be doing at that very second in my life. I only wished that my mom and dad and my twelve brothers and sisters could have been in the room at that momentous time. Oh, they would have been so proud, I thought.

"He touched me and made me whole!" I sang with gusto as I held out the last note as long as my lungs could support it.

Finally, the tone subsided. I took a cleansing breath and opened my eyes, ready to hear what was sure to be praise from the vocal coach. Instead, an awkward silence enveloped the room. My voice instructor adjusted herself in her chair and after a few more moments of silence, she forced a smile. I gritted my teeth and bit my bottom lip as I tried to stay cool and collected. Inside, all I wanted to do was blurt out, "How did I do?" or, "Pretty good, eh?" But what came next were words that impacted my life more than any others.

"Charles, I advise …" She began with her brow furrowed.

My palms were sweating as I waited patiently for the rest of the sentence, anticipating good things such as, "I advise that you pack your bags immediately and sing on Broadway," or, "I advise that you sign a recording contract as soon as you can find an ink pen!"

But rather than gushing praise upon me, I heard something else.

"I strongly advise you NOT to do music," she said in a calm and confident tone.

The expression on her face was as sincere as she could make it. She was giving me her professional advice, and I'm sure she thought she was doing me an enormous favor by sparing me the biggest mistake of my life.

I wanted to defend myself and launch into all the reasons why I was standing there. It wasn't crystal clear to me yet, but I had an overwhelming feeling that somehow in the future God could and would help me use my gift of singing to serve Him. Maybe if she would give me a minute to explain and express my heart, she would change her hasty option. But no words of protest came out of my mouth. I was wounded and my heart sank.

I left the room as crushed as I had ever been. Who would understand the disappointment I was feeling deep inside as my dream was being questioned and causing doubt inside my heart? I was completely committed to being in college. I was so far from home.

There was no way I could let her words defeat me. If I did, I could never look myself in the mirror again. I would forever regret my decision if I threw in the towel. There was no covering the hurt I felt so deeply inside. I was miserably alone, and I only knew of one place to go.

I walked down the hallway and stood at the door of my college advisor, Dr. Larry Roots. I pulled myself together and I tapped on the door. He was a caring, gentle man who had only encouraged me from the first time we met.

"Charles? Come in."

There was no covering the hurt. I sat across from him with tears welling in my eyes. As I suppressed my emotions, I recounted the words that had been spoken to me—words that cut me to the quick.

"Singing is what I am called to do," I said. "I know it in my heart."

As I wiped my tears, my advisor gave me time to collect myself. He took a moment, and then he uttered words that would turn my world back around and place me back on solid ground.

"Never let someone talk you out of what God has placed in you," he said with solid conviction in his voice.

They were Godly words. They were perfect words as if the Holy Spirit had hand-delivered them to my counselor's office. Yes! That was exactly what I needed to hear. To this day I can hear his words in my memory. Rejuvenated, I left his office never to question God's calling on my life again.

Decades later, I'm so blessed because God has used my singing voice and my testimony in thousands of concert performances, revivals, and camp meetings in the United States, England, Scotland, Wales, Norway, Germany, France, Africa, Estonia, Israel, Italy, South America, and Canada.

I dearly love the college where I experienced what it means to hang on tightly to the dream and calling that God has placed in my heart. Thirty-three years after that voice lesson, I was privileged to receive an honorary doctorate in music ministry from Southwest Baptist University. How wonderful it was to accept the honor just a short walk from the very room where I had my first voice lesson. I accepted the degree footsteps away from where I had received some of the wisest counsel of my life.

Honestly, I could have easily held resentment after that experience. I had just left the South where I had seen the ugly side of rejection. In a time of racial struggle and transition, my bitterness could have easily been fanned into a flame. I was determined. I refused to be boxed into where others thought I should be.

Because my upbringing was surrounded by segregation and humiliation, my trust of people didn't come easily. Being obedient to God each day superseded circumstances. Defiance born of my situation as a poor, African-American farm boy in the South slowly turned into the purest Christianity I could muster.

During my unique and adventurous journey to becoming the best person I could ever be, I have learned two things:

Love has to be a lifestyle you live and not a banner you wave.

Love has to be a demonstration and not just a declaration.

When I left my humble beginnings in the South, desire and determination were what drove me. I left my little town of Dermott, Arkansas, and set out to prove something to the world, or to at least all the people who had known me thus far. As a child I was searching for "my voice," or my place in this world. *Where did I fit in?* Little did I realize that searching for my voice meant that I would have to work my way out of my circumstances. My voice … or perhaps we should just call it "my life" … was being trained every step of the way.

After all these years of using my voice, I realize that God had all His plans laid out for me. He had written the song for me to sing before he made the Earth. Today, I also realize that returning to where it all started has taught me as much about my life as did all the decades of singing and traveling the world.

CHAPTER 1

"In The Beginning"

On August 23, 1956, I was the fifth child in a family of thirteen children, and I was born at home just like the other siblings before me. My mom and dad were like most of the farm families who worked in the cotton fields. They were extremely hardworking, God-fearing, and desperately poor—dirt poor. With all those mouths to feed in our little home, we made other poor families look rich! Thankfully, Willie and Ollie Graham may not have had much in their worn and calloused hands, but they had an abundance of unconditional love in their hearts for my family and me.

My parents had several rules for me to live by. They were guidelines that would serve me well: love Jesus, work hard, be honest, respect yourself, respect others, use good manners, and say *Yes, sir* and *Yes, ma'am*. Many of these common life lessons may seem small at first, but combined they become the strong fabric of good character.

My dad worked as a farmhand on a farm in the Arkansas Delta, the fertile ground of the Mississippi River bottomland. My mother and father, like all of the various workers and their families, lived on the farm property. We children rarely left the land on which we were being raised. It was home.

The crude wooden houses that outlined the land were small, unpainted shacks without running water or indoor toilets. They stood in stark contrast to the landowner's nice brick house.

"The day Charles was born, the irrigation pump broke!" the landowner barked his frustrated opinion to my father. "I swear that boy came out screamin' and cryin' and made that pump stop workin'."

It was an absurd accusation to make and a silly thing to blame a newborn baby for, but that's the story that my dad told me and everyone else. The most important piece of farm equipment failing as I cried my first tears as an infant was more than curious happenstance to the farm owner.

My siblings will attest to the fact that breaking the irrigation system set the tone for my existence on the farm. From day one, it seemed that machines didn't like me and so, in return, I haven't gotten along with them.

Of course, machines breaking and my being born have absolutely nothing to do with each other, but it has never stopped my family from associating faulty mechanical objects to the fact that I am around them!

Six decades later, I still can't work on cars or trucks or machines of any kind. I'm very open to learning how to conquer them, but if someone were keeping score, I'd have to say the machines have been winning for years and years. Although I must admit that many years ago when I was struggling in my ministry, I forced myself to replace an alternator in my 1982 Dodge van. Still, if I didn't know better, I'd say that machines of all kinds have an internal hatred built in them just to torment me. In case you think I'm exaggerating, recently I reversed my tractor over my riding lawn mower.

I must brag for a moment that a few months ago I learned to use many of the features on my new cell phone. Like many people, my solutions to conquering my telephone begin by contacting the nearest teenager, niece or nephew who is growing up surrounded by our overwhelming technology or finding a dependable person like my friend Jody at an AT&T store in Tulsa, Oklahoma.

Seeing all the modern conveniences and technological advances in our world today serves as a reminder of all the things I did without as a child living on a cotton field in Southeast Arkansas. The farm had some old tools, as well as a few modern ones for the workers to access and use, but they were mainly for the benefit of the farm owner. My dad could use, run, and fix about any piece of machinery on the farm, but for the most part none of it was ours.

The farmland was a microcosm of the bigger world. What I mean is that land and its borders were our world. I truly didn't know how big the real world was beyond the property line by which we were mostly confined. The farm was our community. It was a village in and of itself, full of multi-generational families.

I had no idea there was a huge world beyond the turn rows, but as I began to notice more and more the shiny cars periodically speeding by on the paved highway, my mind began to wonder, *Who are the people and where they going?*

I began to dream beyond my circumstances.

CHAPTER 2

"The Farm Community"

To understand where I am now, one needs to understand a little more about the world from which I came. Perhaps the stifling isolation in rural Arkansas became the driving force that pushed my desire to escape it.

The hierarchy of our farm community was simple and predictable. The fathers of the farmhand families were the undisputed heads of each household. The mothers were the nurturing authoritarians who kept family order. The grandparents and older generations were the assumed "wise sages" who contributed their strong voices, opinions, life experiences, and moral influence to anyone younger than they.

When children grew tall enough to stand, walk, and drag a cotton sack, it was assumed that they would not only begin working with their family on the farm, but that their work would be a life-long vocation. In my case, it was assumed that I would start working as a child in the cotton fields and work there until I was an old man like the grandfathers who sat on various porches around the farm. When I was old enough to drag a large burlap sack and bend over hundreds of times each day and pick cotton, I was inserted into the Graham family team of laborers.

The workers were a community of citizens brought together by our heritage, our birthplace, and our circumstances. All the families who saw each other in the fields also saw each other after work.

As you picture the large farm and its land that stretched as far as the eye could see, you must understand that our houses were not neatly situated in established enclaves or encircling a cul-de-sac. It was quite the opposite.

Our homes were randomly scattered around the perimeter of the fields; one here, one there; two here; three there. I could run or walk around the land and before long find myself at a friend's home. The community was truly like an extended family. They were like my aunts and uncles, not random strangers that had no connection or concern for me. Everyone watched out for everyone. The old grandmas or grandpas down the road or across the field treated every child within their view as their own flesh and blood. They felt responsible for us and even corrected us if we misbehaved. I'll get to more of that dynamic in the next chapter.

The landowner called the shots. He had everyone's livelihood in his hands. For instance, if the landowner bought another property and felt compelled to have his farm families live on that new land, he would simply announce that we were moving to a new farm. If the dads wanted to continue working, they packed up their families and what few belongings they had, and without question the families moved with the landowner.

The Nelsons, the Berkleys, and the Wests were the farmhand families who always moved with us. As long as I can remember, where the landowner went, my family went with him.

My earliest memories of working for the landowner are memories of chopping cotton, picking cotton, and weeding beans. I vividly recall the early morning dew on the soybean plants that were taller than me. Dad punched a hole in the top of a plastic trash bag for my head to protrude so when I set out into the fields early in the morning, the bag would keep the moisture off of my clothes.

I hated every moment of the work. I was just a little tyke when Dad taught me to chop weeds around the cotton. I was so miserable, and I wanted out of the task and off the farm! One day, I came up with the bad idea of chopping the cotton instead of the weeds, thinking my dad would run me out of the fields and send me back home. That was not a good plan. Instead of being released of my work duties, I got a swift swat on my backside from Dad and his belt. It's amazing how effective a well-placed smack can be, and how it can refocus you to do the right thing as instructed.

Because of the intense and never-ending labor, the season for picking cotton felt as if it lasted forever. When I started, my pay was two dollars a hundred if I picked one hundred pounds of cotton and crammed it into my cotton sack. From age five to my teenage years, I never picked a hundred pounds of cotton without the help of my siblings. My hatred of working in the cotton field kept me from having enough initiative to pick a hundred pounds.

When I tried to pick faster and attempt to make my goal, I would only experience disappointment and anger as the bag was weighed. During the process I tried so hard to convince myself that the nine-foot-long cotton sack contained at least two hundred pounds of cotton by weighing time.

"Sixty-nine pounds," the man said as he placed my sack on the scales.

"What? Sixty-nine pounds?" I questioned.

"That's right."

"Is that all?"

All the sweat and time bent over only earned me the words of a man shouting out how little I had accumulated in my sack. The shout would then be followed by another swat from my dad because I hadn't picked enough.

One day, my dad came home and announced to my mom that because the farm owner had purchased new land, we would be moving to Baxter, Arkansas.

My sharpest memories of the move began in the old house we were forced to call home. The day we arrived where we were to live, Mom began the cleaning process. Everything in our new abode had to be cleaned and ready for our move-in day. We pumped water, scrubbed floors, washed walls, and cleaned windows until the house met my mother's high standards. I'm sure it would have met the standards of the Ritz Carlton Hotel. She could see dirt where no other human could.

The new land sat on the north side of the highway between Dermott and Collins, which put me in walking distance of my Great Uncle Sam and Aunt Nancy. They fit into the community just as we did because everyone was poor. Now, growing up poor does not mean that you grow up unaware of social levels and financial positions of others. And just because you are a child does not mean that you don't see or understand what's going on around you. At least, that's the way it was for me.

I'll give you a simple example. I was a very young boy when we moved to the new farm. I remember walking to my aunt and uncle's house, and on the way I would pass by the large white two-story farm house where there was, and still is, a metal gate that kept most persons out and off the property. In the center of the gate is a small metal figure of a dog—an aluminum piece of ornamentation that the manufacturer thought would be an artistic touch to an otherwise utilitarian, inanimate object. However, to a poor, young black boy like me, that metal figure of a dog on the gate represented more. The image of that dog became a part of my memories and helped to ignite my determination to reach beyond the imaginary gates that had been erected to keep me from attaining greater things.

Intuitively I knew it would take the tenacity and strength of a working dog to extricate myself from the impoverished situation in which I lived. On the other side of that metal gate that kept me and others like me off of the property, the majestic brick farm house reached and stretched into the Southern sky like an unattainable dream.

That's how rich people live! I thought. *Why not me? What must it be to walk up those steps, turn the door handle, and walk right in like I'm somebody?*

I didn't have to be the smartest kid on the farm to know that I didn't want to live in an old, unpainted sharecropper house that sat on cinder blocks.

As I stood at the end of the plantation sidewalk, staring through the chain linked fence that kept me out, I could only dream that someday I would live in a nice house like that and I would meet and befriend people who didn't work with their hands bloodied from toiling in the cotton fields. I wanted so much more, and somehow, someway I was going to change my situation.

Just a few paces from that figure of the dog on the gate, the two-lane highway buzzed with cars and trucks going east and west. As a small boy, I wanted desperately to follow that highway and see where else in the world it would take me. That kind of wanderlust or adventurous thinking was very foreign to most of the adults, who assumed that all of us kids would be naturally relegated to our community of farm workers.

Staying on the farm and going nowhere was ingrained in the thinking of our whole community, who considered it to be the wise and only choice.

Now, as I think back, I can see why the little African-American boy standing outside the plantation gate was considered to be "different." As a child, I began to hear the whispers in our community, in my church, and, of course, in my immediate family.

"There's something different about Charles," I would hear people say. "He's not like the other boys."

I didn't like hearing those comments, but in a way, they were motivating to me. I did not want to fit in and be like all the other kids my age. For the most part, they were content to fit in and follow the path of their parents and their siblings before them. That kind of existence was not going to be a choice for me.

There has been that same gnawing and churning in my soul for most of my life. It wasn't as if I thought I was any better than the next person or any of my siblings. I had an insatiable desire to spread my wings and fly in new, bold, and different directions. It's clear that I didn't appreciate my station in life or my family's station, but I came to realize that God was always in control and His mercies were new each day.

CHAPTER 3

"He Knows His Plans for Me"

Reminiscing about my most formidable years on the farm helps me to understand now that every day, every person, and every experience on that patch of land established a strong foundation for the person I am today. Some might say today that the Grahams were "dirt poor." Being dirt poor and black in the Deep South of the United States came with historical meaning. Prejudice and segregation were prevalent in our country.

A tangible example of that reality happened one afternoon as we were picking cotton and sweating profusely in the hot sun. The landowner and his young grandson stood at the corner of the field watching all us laborers pick cotton. I was a young teenager at the time, and the landowner's grandson was about ten years younger than me.

The contrasts and differences in our lives and lifestyles were stark. I wore second or even third-hand clothes with patches over the knees. He stood nearby wearing a neatly pressed white button-up shirt, new khakis, and a pair of cowboy boots. Keeping the sun off his face was a dapper, wide-brimmed hat that probably cost more money than my family collectively made on that miserably hot day.

The landowner began shouting to the foreman in the distance, "Andrew! Andrew! Andrew!" As he called, I was just a few feet away from the boss, keeping my head down and trying to look as if I were interested in my task and being productive. What sent a shock wave through my heart was what was said next.

"Paw-paw, them *niggers* don't hear you," the young white boy said, as if he were referring to a herd of cattle in the field.

It was the first time I'd ever heard the derogatory name that African-Americans had heard over the decades. It was not a shout. It was the matter-of-fact tone and vocabulary of a young boy talking to his grandpa.

Like a knife, the child's "n" word pierced my heart. It was the first time I had heard it said about me, and it did not make me feel good. It was hurtful and demeaning. But knowing what was said about me was not as hurtful as hearing a word like that directed at my family and me for the first time. Words have meaning, and words can be more powerful and more damaging than any explosive ordinance if aimed at a vulnerable heart or mind. When I think of the power of words, I often think about first moments of recorded history in the Bible. God spoke things into existence. That's how powerful holy words from a holy God can be. If we are to be his servants operating as ambassadors to a fallen world, how important it must be to watch our words. They can heal, or they can steal. They can mend, or they can tear to shreds. They can restore, or they can damage beyond repair.

The dark shadow of hurtful words and attitudes was where the Grahams began. Circumstances had us bound and placed in the back of the social line in the South. It would be my quest to free myself from the circumstances that had me chained to a dead end road. The climb up and out of the dark shadows would take character and determination. It would also take a belief in my heart that God knew the plans that he had for me, plans to give me hope and future.

Family, relatives, friends, teachers, and people of my community helped to impact my personality, my attitudes, my beliefs, and my character. To give the reader a better picture of my humble beginnings, it is helpful to understand the accommodations I called home.

A typical morning for the Grahams started with Mom waking us up way too early. It did not matter our age, my brothers and sisters and I were expected to participate in the cooking, cleaning, and taking care of the younger siblings as Mom went off to work the fields.

Let me attempt to paint a mental picture of the abode that my mother was leaving behind as she hurried off to work each morning. Imagine if you will, a wooden structure covered in red composite shingles. We jokingly called it our imitation brick house. Now, imagine the square wooden structure sitting up on a foundation of blocks. Set that house at the edge of hundreds of acres of cotton and beans and you'll begin to get a picture of the four-room house where I grew up.

People often ask me how many bedrooms were in the little house. I laugh and tell them that it was a four-room house with eight to ten people, so every room was a bedroom.

The older I got, the more I began to understand how simple my farmhouse was. Besides the fact that it had no indoor plumbing, it did not have heating or air conditioning either. When I describe the house in which I grew up to people today, I usually get a strange look when I say that I always knew what the weather was outside.

"When it rained outside, it was raining inside. If it was snowing outside, it was snowing inside."

My mother was and still is a woman of innovation, so it was second nature to her to find solutions to things that poor persons must endure. A famous Greek philosopher once said, *Necessity is the mother of invention.* My dear mother embodies that ancient saying. Her problem-solving skills were developed over her years as a child, teen, and married adult who had to learn to live with very little. She saw the cracks in the interior walls, and where there was a crack, there had to be something to cover it. Where there was a need, she fought hard to meet it. Whether it was cracks in the wall or cracks in our character, Mom was sure to do her best to make repairs.

It was not like it is today when the builder quickly covers the interior walls using sheetrock. Mother's creative solution was to scrape together a few dollars, find some discounted wallpaper, and cover the walls. When there was no flour to make wallpaper paste, Mother would neatly stretch out the paper and have us cut small squares out of the paper. Rather than adhere the paper with paste, we would push thumbtacks into the middle of the paper square and then nail the squares onto the wall. It was obviously not as efficient as wallpaper adhered to the walls, but her effective use of paper and thumbtacks did give us the protection and the decor the walls needed. It made for an interesting design, and I'm sure the wallpaper manufacturer would have never thought of such an application. Without paper paste, my Mother thought of it immediately. There was a creative art to her innovation and also a sensible practicality. Necessity drove her toward ingenuity.

The only running water the house had was when one of us kids ran to the pump and ran back. That was our definition of "running" water. Doing chores included lugging the water buckets each day from the outside pump to the kitchen. Our routine was to fetch the water in two or three buckets and then carry them into the house. Oh, I should mention that there was no sink in the kitchen like in today's homes. We just set the buckets full of water onto the counter.

This was our routine and responsibility day after day. Regardless of the weather, in and out we would go. When I made the trek from the house to the pump, I would think, "There must be a better way to do this!"

Next to the pump was an old coffee can with a little water in it to prime the pump. If the last sibling whose turn it was had forgotten to leave some priming water in the old can, that meant I had to take the coffee can to a ditch nearby to fill it with priming water. It was not the kind of chore I could ignore. No water in the house meant a spanking for me!

Next to our house was one of the longest flowing bodies of water in the world. There were tons of non-drinkable water flowing right by me every minute of every day in the Bayou Bartholomew, but none of that muddy current was helping me get water into the house.

Once I primed the pump and got the fresh water pumped into the bucket, I had to carry the heavy bucket back to the house and provide water for drinking, cooking, washing, or whatever. I think of that process now when I conveniently turn the handle of one of my indoor sinks, tubs, or showers. Thank God for indoor plumbing!

As if hauling the water inside from the outside pump was not enough of a pain, silt would settle in the bottom of the buckets, and Mother would have to thoroughly clean each bucket using Purex bleach. As the poisonous chlorine did its work on the silt, Mother would make sure the water buckets were placed high and safely atop the refrigerator to keep the kids and me from accidentally drinking dangerous water.

Each of us older siblings would moan and complain about the job, but we dutifully took our turns collecting the fresh water from the pump, and the daily chore taught us about family responsibility. I will say that the duty of providing fresh water also provided fresh family drama.

You see, Mother's commandment was,

"Never go to bed if the buckets are empty," she said in a voice that dripped with serious consequences.

I can still hear her voice today. She made it clear with the tone of her words that the rule should never be broken. I later figured out that her rule was not just about convenience as one might think, but it was also about safety.

"Can't we go one night without full buckets, Momma?"

"No! What if there's a fire in the house tonight?" she cautioned.

"Fire?" I asked, because that had never occurred to me.

"That's right. If fire catches hold of this old wooden house, it would be the end of us."

With that image planted in my head, I imagined the whole house burning down with my family inside, and of course the blame would be put squarely on me!

Mother knew how to train us as she also exercised quite often her motherly art of planting some fear in our hearts and minds. Her worrisome words of caution weren't unfounded. Fire was a huge concern since our shack-of-a-house was as dry as kindling—especially during the hot Southern Arkansas summers.

The water bucket rule was so imposing and so serious that even as toddlers it was on the minds of every Graham child. And you can be assured that if one of us forgot the most important chore of the house, every last one of the other siblings would join the chorus of tattletales and sing to high heaven!

"Mother! The bucket's empty!"

"Whose turn is it?"

"Charles forgot again, Momma."

"Charles!"

"He said he filled it, but he didn't. It's empty, Momma."

You see, if one of us was upset with a sister or brother, the old bucket tattletale was a clever way of seeing that a sibling got some payback! We all knew that leaving the bucket dry meant a guaranteed whippin'.

Believe it or not, there was another very irritating rule that Mother dreamed up when it came to the precious water bucket. I called it the "last drink" rule.

"Whoever takes the last drink out of the bucket is the person who has to go to the pump and fill the bucket back up!" Mom reminded us.

I hated the "last drink" rule! As would be expected, the Graham children developed techniques to dodge the "last drink" rule.

We would pick up the bucket and swirl the last ounces around, carefully measuring just how much we could consume without drinking the last few drops. If we took the last swallow, we had to go fetch a fresh bucket of water again.

"Momma, Charles left the bucket empty!"

"No, I didn't!"

"Did too!"

"Did not! There's enough for one more drink."

"Barely a swallow."

"It's in there," I debated.

"Stop your arguing," Mother shouted in her most authoritative tone. "Whoever's next, go fill the bucket."

One summer day, I accidentally created a legendary moment that to this day is recalled during family gatherings. It all started with a simple but delicious piece of candy. Rarely did the Graham children get candy, but on one particular hot summer day we all got candy and ate it as we played together. The candy was very good, but it made me very thirsty. My mouth was dry, and I needed immediate relief.

I bolted from the front yard into the house, leaving the other kids to play without me for a moment. I dashed into the kitchen to get a cold drink of water. It was one of my first life lessons about how sometimes when we want something so desperately, we tend to shut off our minds!

The bucket was sitting higher than usual, but the only thing on my childish mind was to grab, drink, and get back to playing outside. I grabbed a kitchen chair, and using it as a step stool, I then stepped onto the table to reach the bucket on top of the refrigerator.

I shook the bucket, and there was just enough water to quench my thirst. Because it wasn't my turn to collect water, I quickly accessed the moment; I would drain the bucket quickly without anyone seeing me, and no person would be the wiser.

Hastily I tipped the bucket of water into the old tin dipper and in one gulp I swallowed it as quickly as I had retrieved it.

"Ahhhhhhhhhhhhhh! Purex!" I shouted.

It only took a second for my taste buds to inform me that I had consumed several ounces of poisonous chlorine water! Mother assumed she had set the tainted water up high enough to keep any of the children from accidentally drinking it. As fast as my legs could carry me, I burst out of the house.

"Mother," I choked, "I ... drank..." <Spit> <Gag> "I ... drank..." I tried to utter the words, but my mouth was under attack from the burning Purex.

I could not form even one more word. I gagged and I spat some more ... and then, I gagged some more. In a flash, Mom disappeared into the house. Meanwhile, my siblings were standing around, wondering if on this fateful day they were going to see the death of a brother, either by choking on poison, or by whipping by our mother!

The back door burst back open, and Mother ran toward me with unusual speed. In one hand she had a scoop of lard that she had fetched from the red box in the kitchen. She forced that lard down my throat like she was stuffing the wrong end of a Thanksgiving turkey. Just thinking of all that lard going in my burning mouth and traveling down my throat was enough to make me sick.

As I swallowed and gagged the slick, nasty pig fat, my stomach revolted and rejected the unwelcome visitor! I threw up like I had never thrown up before. Oh, I was sick. After attending to the immediate need and seeing that I would live through my stupidity, Mother then took a belt to me for not being careful.

I wish I could say that the rest of that summer day faded quietly into the sunset, but it did not. Later that same day I went to my Aunt Nancy's house. My throat was still raw from the chlorine going in and the chlorine and lard going back out. Naturally, I began telling her the traumatizing story of how I had accidentally consumed Purex.

"Purex?"

I hardly got the story started before my poor aunt was diving for the lard to shove down my throat!

"No, Aunt Nancy!"

"Take it! Eat it!"

Aunt Nancy grabbed my arm and shoved lard at me with force. My lips slammed shut like two iron doors. Nothing was coming in—especially not lard.

"Eat the lard, or you're gonna die!"

As I remember all the struggle and calculations I had to go through in order to avoid drinking that last drop of water, it reminds me of the weakness in the character and behavior of people today as we take such care to avoid obligations. If only we could learn to thankfully drink the last drop and graciously fill the next bucket of water for others.

I observe how much things in life have changed over the years regarding parental discipline. Rules in the family were made for a purpose. They were put in place, and we were required to obey them. Rules kept us healthy and safe, and they taught necessary disciplines for our life-long survival and character building. If I messed up and broke any of Mom or Dad's rules, a whipping on my backside quickly followed. It may seem primitive or harsh today, but it was a process of teaching me that my actions can have painful consequences. Even in my thirstiest times of need when I believe I see a quick solution, it is wise to see God's wisdom before I take a hasty drink of something that I feel will solve a desperate issue. I thank God that he says to come to Him when I am thirsty. He promises me living water to sustain me. For his children, the water is always cool and refreshing and waiting to give us strength that sustains us.

CHAPTER 4

"God Gave Us Imaginations"

The Grahams were a close family whether we wanted to be or not. I love my brothers and sisters, and although our little house was a very crowded house, I would not have changed a thing. Our home was like my early childhood—simple and chocked-full of humility. When you are young and poor, you really don't know how poor you are because, frankly, that life is all you know.

Our house was situated close to the main barn, where the farm implements were stored. I sometimes reflect back to those innocent days, and I start with a vision of my hard-working dad—a model work hand.

Dad was dependable and invaluable to the entire operation. I would call him our living example of what hard work means. My dad could not provide many material possessions, but he made up for it with unconditional love.

Mom and Dad nurtured an environment of close relationships between my brothers and sisters and me. I appreciate every day the friendship and camaraderie that I still have with each of my siblings. With so many kids already in the house, I never had to ask the neighborhood kids to join me in a game. There was plenty of imagination and playmates to provide us something to do.

When you have more siblings than you need to field a baseball team, you always have enough participants for just about any game a kid can think of. However, I must say that it could be an added benefit at times to have not only so many children in my immediate family, but also all the kids in our unique neighborhood as well. Games like tag were epic!

Everyone watched over each other as if we were related. People these days talk about "the community" in general terms, but in Boydell, Baxter, and Dermott, "the community" was real and tangible.

The community was our family. Neighbors were caretakers, caregivers, and self-appointed guardians. Any adult could and would discipline any one of us. It was just understood that if there was a neighborhood kid in the vicinity, the nearest adult assumed parental rights, and that meant over all children. To make the connection even stronger, the same people in the houses were also the people who made up the entire congregation of our little country church, so there was no escaping some kind of parental authority no matter where I roamed.

As I walk the dirt road these days and reminisce, I can still hear their voices in my mind. The community is still such a part of who I am today as I develop long-held friendships around the world. In Baxter, the heat of the long, hot summers, the sounds of the country, and the most powerful smells of Southern life fill my memories. There is something so unique about the aroma of flowers and grass in the Deep South. The freshly plowed dirt of the fields adds a rich scent to the fresh air. That was the community I was privileged to wake up to every morning of my youth.

Inside our respective farmhouses, there were some similarities, but I liked to think that the Grahams had many unique features. I'll give you a few examples. My mother created a particular scent inside our home that continues to take me back to my childhood on the farm. It's an aroma that I will never get tired of—the smell of her wonderful homemade biscuits that she made for us every morning.

Out of all the magnificent dishes Mom would create, it was her mouth-watering biscuits that made her famous in our house and in our community. Now, making sure the biscuits were baked properly, however, was not just my mother's responsibility. It became a family responsibility.

When her delectable creations were pulled from the oven and ready to consume, it was a little piece of heaven in a pan for all the Graham family. But there was another reason the biscuits became a family affair, and it was not due to just the incredible taste.

Because of the large amount of biscuits Mother had to prepare, she used a long biscuit pan that had to be watched by one of us. The problem was getting that extra long biscuit pan into a normal sized oven. One of us Graham kids always had to keep a watchful eye on the biscuits as they were browning because when it came time, one of us had to turn the pan to keep the process going smoothly. If the precious biscuits were somehow neglected and burned, it was a whipping offense. And to make matters worse, the offending child responsible for the biscuits being charred had to scrape the burnt portion off the biscuits so they could still be consumed. Throwing out burnt biscuits would have been almost criminal and definitely considered a waste.

In hindsight, becoming a part of the cooking process benefited me. I'm sure I took for granted Mom's instruction as a child, but as I cook today for friends and visitors, I realize she was constantly passing on her kitchen wisdom and expertise to me. Mom's culinary knowledge was passed down from her mother and her mother before her. It is a huge matter of pride for her now that many of her kids can cook well.

Having lots of siblings wasn't always a bad thing. We loved each other, and though we had our disagreements now and again, we never let an argument drive a wedge between us. I remember the joy we derived just from being in each other's company.

Imagination was never in short supply when the young siblings and I played our "Kill the Giant" game. Wanda, Joyce, the young ones, and I would pretend that at any given moment, over the horizon would come the biggest, meanest giant ever to walk the earth. We imagined that he was a very vicious giant, who was coming to our house to eat us for his next meal. When you believe a giant is coming to eat you, you have to have a plan. Our plan was to fill buckets with household items such as oil, washing powder, and Clorox. When the giant would pick us up and hold us over his open mouth, the plan was to drop our bucket in his mouth, and he would hopefully eat the contents and not us.

Because we came up with such an ingenious plan to save the world from the horrible giant, the President of the United States would invite us to the White House and give us a hero's welcome.

I could picture us driving up to the beautiful White House in a limousine. What a sight that would be for the president to see the heroic Graham kids piling out of the limo and scampering up the stairs! I was convinced that he would commend us and give us gifts for bravery such as a new house and new cars for each of us.

Even in the games and stories I imagined, the theme was about me going far away from home. I had giants and obstacles in my life to fight through.

I often imagined leaving the farm and living somewhere far away in a house surrounded by beautiful lawns and sidewalks. I knew without a doubt that rich people did not have to go to the murky creek or swim in muddy old Bayou Bartholomew. I had never seen them there, so that had to be a fact. I was certain that the truly blessed families in the world had their own swimming pools that were clean and convenient.

One morning I awoke and decided to take matters into my own hands. I was determined to do something about our sad little lawn that had no character, no personality, and almost no grass. With all the children's feet going back and forth, there was never much of a lawn. So there was only one thing to do as far as I was concerned—transform the front yard and build our own swimming pool!

For those of you who know me well, building a swimming pool might seem like the last thing I would propose since I was deathly afraid of water, but I think I was more intrigued by the fantastic idea of having a pool.

"Where shall we build our new pool?" the kids debated.

"The side yard!"

"The back yard!"

"Nope. It'll be right in the front yard for everyone to see," I said. "We are going to show the world that we are moving up."

My brothers and sisters loved the idea as I continued to verbally expand my vision.

"Best part; you can stand on the front porch and dive right in!"

That induced some cheers and excitement in the siblings. Diving off the porch was a unique idea that no one had ever thought of. The notion that we could simply run out the front door on a sultry summer day and splash into the water excited everyone.

"And it's not going to be a little pool. I say we dig and dig until our pool takes up the whole front yard!"

"That's the greatest idea ever! Yes!" the kids cheered in agreement.

With everyone enthusiastically on board, my imagination grew. I envisioned building a wonderful wooden walkway that would gently wind over the water. No one anywhere would have such an attractive feature in front of his or her home. It would be a one-of-a-kind.

It was time to set our scheme in motion. Mom and Dad left for work just like clockwork, so our construction was about to begin.

"This is going to be great!

"Our very own swimming pool!"

We all were giddy and determined and full of excitement. Our property would be the only homestead on our dirt road, or perhaps anywhere, that had a swimming pool for a front yard!

We scarfed down our breakfast, cleaned up the kitchen, and then dashed outside to assume our duties. James fetched the wheelbarrow.

"Joyce! We'll map out the pool," I suggested.

"Okay!"

"Everyone else, start scraping the grass off the yard. We have a lot of digging to do!"

I knew Joyce would take the task seriously. She and I mapped out the border of the pool. The others kept scraping grass, digging dirt, and hauling it away. The little ones were so proud to be doing their part. It was truly a family affair and an event that we would never forget.

Suddenly, I stopped scraping grass and stood back to assess the progress. My back was hurting, and my hands were immediately getting blisters. My plan to build a pool was fully engaged, and I should have been full of joy. But when I stretched and took a deep breath to scan our excavation of the front lawn, all I could see was a complete disaster. The yard looked horrible. The sight hit me like a ton of bricks. My exuberance turned to a sickening feeling in the pit of my stomach.

"Oh, no! Oh, no, no, no!" I cried out.

The busy little Graham workers heard my outburst. I'm sure they could read my face. But what they could not see was the remorse stretching from the top of my head to the bottom of my guilty feet!

"Stop! Stop digging!" I shouted, with a tone that carried all the fear and regret pouring from my heart. "Stop! Everyone, stop!"

Joyce turned and asked, "What's the matter Charles?"

"Uh-oh," one of my brothers said.

"Look what we've done!"

"What? We just did what you told us to do."

"I've made a big mistake," my voice cracked with a sound that let each of the kids know that it was something really bad we had done.

In a matter of minutes our mom and dad's lawn had become a complete disaster! What little grass my parents had tried to grow was lying in a dirt pile in the backyard. Piles of soil yet to be hauled away lay around the edge of the Graham "swimming pool," acting as mounds of incriminating evidence that would get us all whippings for the rest of our lives.

"What's wrong, Charles?"

"Put it back."

"What?"

"Put it back! All of it! Put it back the way it was!"

"That's impossible."

"Are you crazy?"

"It was a bad idea," I admitted.

"I knew it! I thought we would get in trouble," a brother moaned.

"What about all our work?"

"What about our pool?"

"What about jumping off the front porch?"

"Forget everything I said. Put it back. Put it all back before Mom and Dad get here and kill us all!"

"You've gone and done it now, Charles."

"We're dead."

Obviously, I had not thought this one through. Collective panic covered all the faces of the Graham excavation crew. They knew what I knew. If we did not get the dirt packed back into place, we were all facing the most severe wrath of our parents.

As I watched my brothers and sisters scramble feverishly to repair the widespread front yard damage, it couldn't get dark fast enough for me!

"Please, Lord, let the sun go down faster?" I begged.

Okay, my faith was big, but not that big—not Joshua-in-the-Bible big. He could request the sun and moon to stand still. I took a shot that God could answer my prayer and cause the sun to speed up. I scraped and scraped the dirt. I prayed and prayed, but the sun stayed on its daily path, and a little while later Mom and Dad got home. If there had been a place to run and hide, I know a bunch of Graham children who would probably still be missing!

"Bend over!" Dad said gruffly.

I prayed like never before. This was going to be an epic whippin'—one for the Graham history books. You know it's a bad whippin' when your parent whips your backside, and with every whack he or she utters parts of a sentence. It went something like this:

"You'll <WHACK> think <WHACK> harder <WHACK> before you <WHACK> go <WHACK> scraping <WHACK> the <WHACK> grass off <WHACK> the <WHACK> yard <WHACK> again!" <WACK> Daddy declared with anger. "Won't you?" <WHACK>

"Yes, sir!"

"And one more just because!" <WHACK>

Never did my father speak truer words. I would indeed "think" before I rallied my siblings to tear up anything in the future.

CHAPTER 5

"Family Life"

Before the readers of my story cast too much judgment upon my parents for their discipline, I stand in their defense as I try for a moment to put myself in their place. Yes, they instituted a strong sense of right and wrong, but with so many mouths to feed, they had to keep us disciplined for our own good. They were determined to equip me and my brothers and sisters with the tools to make it in this world. Discipline to understand right and wrong was a bedrock principle. Love God was number one, but making the right choice to do the right thing was very important.

In the shadow of the strict environment of rules, there was still a sweet love we had for each other. It is a joy to look back and consider those wonderful days full of imagination and possibilities that were birthed out of poverty, because I know now how rich we were to have parents who cared for us and loved us unconditionally.

There is a wonderful humility about living in rural Arkansas. You live off the land and work your fingers to the bone to provide food for yourself and your family. Once in a while, I'm reminded of my humble beginnings when I sit down to a meal. I have a profound respect for where we get our food. I've seen firsthand how items on our dinner plate start with food grown in the family garden.

We didn't grow our food because it was some sort of healthy alternative to shopping in a supermarket; we grew it because it was how we could afford to eat! For me, a chicken dinner is "seasoned" with memories of life on our farm.

Sometimes, when Aunt Nancy came to visit us, it meant she was going to kill a chicken. When she shouted her orders to line up around the house, it was our cue to space ourselves evenly around the perimeter. We all understood without being told that Auntie intended to kill a chicken for dinner.

Why did we have to line up around the house? Because when Aunt Nancy wringed the neck of the poor fowl, the chicken's body ran wildly around our property, and if it got under the house, that meant that one of us would have to crawl under the house and pull it out.

"Everybody line up around the house!" Aunt Nancy would shout to the kids.

"Aww. Everybody?" I complained.

"You too, Charles."

To this day, few things creep me out more than a headless chicken running wildly. I can still see those poor chickens flapping their wings and running speedily with absolutely no purpose or reason! When they lost their heads and ran around the yard erratically—sometimes right at me—it was my personal horror movie.

My job, like the rest of the siblings', was to position myself along the bottom edge of the porch so the headless chicken could not dash under the house. Each Graham child's job was to guard as much space as he or she could.

Imagine if you will, eight or ten soccer goalies keeping an out-of-control ball from entering the net. Come to think of it, maybe that's another reason I never played soccer.

The saying *Running like a chicken with its head cut off* is based on actual fact. Once that head is severed, the chicken body runs here, there, and everywhere!

A lasting effect of killing chickens helped to develop quite an aversion to eating any meat that had been killed on our property. I hated hog killin' day. I hated chicken pluckin' day. I hated fish cleaning day. I don't mean I was a vegetarian. I would eat meat from the clean, white paper like the kind a butcher provided at Mr. Wells' grocery store, but if I saw the disgusting, bloody brown paper that wrapped up the butchered animals from our farm, that's when I would surrender and avoid the meat at the dinner table altogether.

As I got older, life was increasingly noisier and active at my house. We still had to live a simple life due to the fact that Mom and Dad were still raising lots of kids. A few of my brothers moved out, but it was still a daunting challenge trying to keep us all in clothing and keep food in our stomachs.

After gathering around the table for a meal and quickly cleaning and putting away the dishes, we gathered in the front room to watch a movie on our black-and-white TV. As a reminder to my younger readers, I'll mention that there was a time when televisions were not in color, they didn't have remote controls, and there were only three or four channels ... if you were fortunate enough to live where the television signals were strong.

Eventually, the channel knob broke. Of course, the issue was quickly remedied by an old pair of vice grips from Dad's toolbox that he attached to the front of the TV. Once the TV was turned on and the vice grips had tuned us to the correct channel, one of us had to go outside to turn the television antenna so the channel could find its optimum reception.

"It's all snowy!" we grumbled.

I'm not sure that kids today understand what I mean when I say that there was "snow" on the screen. Suffice it to say, the bad reception looked like snow blocking the view of the images that the TV network had intended for us to watch.

"Go turn the antenna," Dad grunted.

One of my older brothers would go outside to turn the antenna as one of my sisters would stand in the doorway to relay the messages regarding reception on the TV screen.

"Go back!"

"There!"

"No. Wait! You had it! Go back!"

"Wait. Don't move!"

My brother kept turning the aerial, hoping to hear someone say that the old black-and-white TV had a picture on it that was bearable to watch.

"A little more!"

"No, no! There. Wait!"

"Go back like you had it!"

It had to be frustrating to be the brother turning the antenna.

"There! That's it! Don't move it!"

We would let out a big cheer and scream that the picture was decent enough to watch.

The person moving the antenna and the relay girl would run back inside and find their place in front of the

TV set to watch whatever was clear enough. My dad's favorite shows were any Westerns that happened to be on. Sunday afternoons we watched Disney movies. For me, I liked a large diet of Elvis movies because I enjoyed the music in his films. Favorite movies that got all of us a little more excited were films with Jerry Lewis in them. Movies like "The Nutty Professor," "The Disorderly Orderly," and "Cinderfella" made us all laugh.

I loved it when we all piled into the old living room to watch. One day, Mom and Dad changed the whole feel of the living room when they surprised us and told us that they bought a sofa that turned into a bed.

We were thrilled at the news and even more excited when the delivery truck arrived before Mom and Dad had returned from work. The nice gentleman who delivered the sleeper sofa demonstrated to all of us kids just how to operate the sofa and turn it into a bed. It was a beautiful thing to behold! The backrest reclined to an even position with the seat cushions.

"I'm sleeping on it!"

"Me too!"

"All of us can sleep on it!"

Considering the fact that we often had four or five of us in one bed, the thought of another place to sleep was exciting.

We all thought that the sleeper couch in the living room was the most brilliant invention we had ever seen. There was always a need for another place to sleep more bodies, and a sofa bed was a great solution.

The deliveryman carefully returned the couch to its normal seating position and left the house. In an instant we had that couch reclined into a bed. For some inexplicable reason, out of the blue, James did the most random act of stupidity I had ever seen. He actually cut the new couch with a knife. We don't exactly know why. It's just what happened. We were all shocked as we looked at the cut along the seam of the couch.

"Fold it up! If Mom and Dad see that, we're dead!"

We folded the couch back into its sitting position once more.

At first, the cut was the width of his knife, and if left alone, it wasn't noticeable—or so we hoped. But, the plastic material betrayed us. Soon the cut began to run. The slit in the plastic grew bigger and bigger to where it was very noticeable.

"Keep your feet off it, and we can all enjoy sitting on it. Take turns, now!" Mother laid down the rules when she got home to see her beautiful new purchase.

I don't remember how severe the punishment was for James, but I know how severe it was for me. I got another memorable whippin' because my sweet mother had saved her hard-earned money to buy the special sleeper sofa. The careless and inexplicable act of my little brother was a reflection on me because I wasn't paying enough attention to the little one.

The couch stayed in the house, despite the knife wound. When guests came to visit, we made sure multiple children sat and hid the cut in the cushion.

CHAPTER 6

"Neighborhood Watch"

On weekends, the Graham family would travel into town to buy groceries or things needed from the department store or hardware store. There was always a reason to go into town. Now, before you get a picture of ten kids and two parents packing the car seats and hanging off the edge of a flat bed pickup truck like the Beverly Hillbillies, we actually had a car—an old four-door car. We were pressed into a worn-out sedan. Actually, it wasn't too bad because we decided that we would alternate which children got to go to town on Saturday. A privileged six or seven of us got to get off the farm and shop in town with Mom and Dad, and the remainder of the family took turns staying at home with the little ones.

There was no such concept as staying home alone. I mean, even when I was left to watch the babies, we were never alone. You see, when you lived in my farm community, you could bet that every family was either related, or they felt as if they knew you so well they would act like blood relatives. Blood relatives, or those who think they are, treat you differently. They think they have charge over you and can parent you and tell you what to do.

Miss Melvina Tucker was affectionately—or maybe I should say respectfully—known as "Miss Mel." If there were ever an award given to the person who invented and perfected the idea of a neighborhood watch program, Miss Mel would be the spokesperson and face of the organization. She wasn't a relative, but you would never know by the way she treated my siblings and me.

Miss Mel lived in a little house behind our house and just past our garden. She knew every man, woman, and child by first, middle, and last name. She had a firm grasp on each child's likes, dislikes, and temperament. Because she was old and beyond her productive working years, her daily, self-appointed job was to watch over the collective family members like a mother hen protecting her chicks. Or maybe, I should say a mother lion roaming around with watchful eyes glued to every move the wayward cubs would make.

Today, it would be the feeling you get when you walk into a department store. You look around and see security cameras in every corner. It's a protection that retail uses for the bad guys, but sometimes it makes you feel like the bad guy. That's the feeling we got with Miss Mel. If any of the kids in the neighborhood broke a rule or did anything risky or challenging or something like digging a homemade swimming pool in the front yard, Miss Mel was the eighty-year-old chief inspector and supreme tattletale. When my parents got home, she would grab her walking stick and trek from her house to ours.

"What now, Miss Mel?" Dad asked.

"It's Charles."

"What did the boy do now?"

"Charles let the children play in the road today," she announced as if she were broadcasting the nightly news.

"That boy! I've told him," Mother agreed with frustration.

"And, half the time I don't think he was keepin' an eye on the children at all."

"Charles Graham! Get in here."

"Yes, ma'am?"

"You let the kids play in the road?" Dad joined in.

"No, sir." I lied.

Things got awkward quickly.

"Then, I guess Miss Mel is lying," he challenged.

Even though I had been trained that I should never dispute the word of an adult, I answered, "No, sir."

That reply earned me a glare from Mom, Dad, and Miss Mel. Finally, Dad broke the silence.

"So, Miss Mel is lying?"

"No, sir."

"Did the kids play in the road?"

"No, sir."

"Sounds like you're saying she's lying."

"No, sir."

That was it. Dad had given me enough opportunity to come clean, but the simple truth was not going to cross my lips that day. I hated that moment. I knew exactly what was going to happen. Methodically, Dad took off his belt. The sound of the belt being unbuckled sent that feeling down my spine.

After Miss Mel witnessed the whipping, she felt her civic duty had been accomplished, so she turned and went to the next house to tell on the next child. Now, you're getting a picture of why I developed a bit of disdain for the old gal and her self-proclaimed neighborhood watch program.

As time passed, Miss Mel and I had a running, unspoken feud. One spring day, Mother took the siblings and me to the garden that separated our homes.

"You plant the beans."

"Yes, ma'am."

"You plant okra."

"Yes, ma'am."

"I'll plant the corn, Mother," I volunteered with a bit of devious calculation in mind. My theory was that I could build a wall of visual protection along the edge of the garden that would completely conceal any of my activity that failed to reach Miss Mel's high standards. A robust wall of corn stalks would surely keep Miss Mel from spying on me!

"Okay. You plant the corn, Charles."

"Yes, ma'am."

"Now, do it right—three kernels in the ground at a time."

"Three kernels. Yes, ma'am."

"Not two, not five … three kernels."

"Yes, ma'am."

I commenced my planting duty, but when Mother was not looking my way, I planted a fistful of corn kernels in the hole, not just three measly little kernels. The next few weeks I watched with anticipation as my corn stalk fortress began to grow. I was certain that I had devised the perfect plan, and I prayed and asked God to help the corn grow together nice and tight and tall in order to block Miss Mel's view.

What I hoped would be an impenetrable wall of leafy green stalks turned out to be a flimsy row of slender stalks that blocked nothing—especially the eyes of such a seasoned old neighborhood watcher. On one occasion, one of my bad decisions sent me straight into the waiting arms of Miss Mel. My little brother James—six kids down from me—was one of the little ones under my distracted care. One of us accidentally dropped an egg on the kitchen floor, and it cracked open. Now, when food was a precious commodity and there was always a hungry child in the house, wasting an egg was a big deal.

"I'll eat it," James said innocently.

"No! You're not going to eat a broken egg off the floor," we protested.

"Why not?" James wondered.

"Let him eat it," I jumped in.

"I dare ya, James."

Someone scraped up the broken egg, and James consumed it like a champ.

"Oh, no!"

We were all about to gag watching James eat the slimy yoke and egg white.

"He did it!"

"James ate it!"

"I'll eat another one!" James said.

Being the ornery big brother in charge and in control of all activity, I got little James a cup and broke not one, but two and then three raw eggs for our little egg-eater.

"He's eating them! Nooooo!"

The kids and I laughed and laughed to see our innocent little brother taking the dare to the limit—his limit. But then, everything changed.

"Ohhhhhhhhhh. I'm sleepy," James groaned.

"Sleepy?" I wondered.

James began to crumble. He wanted to lie down, he told us in a mumble.

"I'm sleepy."

"Look at his eyes," someone shouted.

"His eyes are blue."

Sure enough, I convinced the others and myself that the whites of little James's eyeballs were turning a strange shade of blue.

One of the kids shouted, "James is dying! You killed him, Charles!"

"He's not dying!"

"Just look at 'im, Charles."

"Oh, no. Keep him awake!"

"Don't let him close his eyes."

"He's dying"

Fear gripped all of us as we stood around our "dying" baby brother.

"That was a really dumb idea, Charles."

"You killed James."

The kids started turning on me.

"I did not!"

"Did too."

"James! James!" I pleaded, "Don't go to sleep."

I shook him. We all shook James as we kept talking to him, trying to keep him conscious. There was no changing his will to sleep.

"This isn't working. Let's get him outside."

I carried James outside into the fresh air.

"Miss Mel!" someone shouted. "We gotta take him to Miss Mel!"

"She'll know what to do," the kids agreed.

As much as I hated to admit it, the kids were right. So I carried James through the garden, and we marched through my pathetic corn stalk fortress wall. The Graham entourage of kids made its way to the front porch of the queen of our neighborhood watch. To make the awkward situation a bit more tense and uncomfortable,

Miss Mel was on her front porch entertaining all of her family.

"What have you gone and done now?" Miss Mel asked.

"What happens when you eat raw eggs?" I asked the curious Miss Mel.

"My brother used to eat a raw egg every day before he went running," Miss Mel replied.

"James ate one."

Sleepy James was wide-awake due to the excitement.

"You gave it to me," James chimed in and betrayed me.

"You fed that child raw eggs?"

"He liked them."

"You know what's a comin', Charles?"

"Wait, Miss Mel. If the eggs won't hurt him, why are you giving me a whippin'?"

"'Cause you didn't know they wouldn't hurt him, but you fed them to him anyhow."

Miss Mel picked up a switch that she kept handy on her porch. After several stinging blows to my backside, Miss Mel finished her warnings to me.

"Next time, you'll watch that baby closer in case he eats something that might kill him! Now, go on home and stay in the house. Feedin' a baby raw eggs! Ain't you got any sense, Charles?"

The Graham siblings and I traipsed back through the garden and into the safety of our house. In my best threatening voice, I warned them.

"Nobody tell Mom and Dad what happened."

There was silence as I looked for a loyal brother or sister to back me up.

"We won't have to tell. Miss Mel will tell them before anybody gets a chance."

My heart sank. You can guess what I received in return for my bad judgment. But, before you draw too many negative conclusions, I must make it very clear how much we all truly appreciated Miss Mel—not the whippings or being told on, but for whom she was. I would hate for one's impression of Miss Mel to be negative in any way.

Yes, Miss Mel was a disciplinarian. She wanted the rules to be kept and never bent or broken. She enforced and re-enforced the rules that my mother had placed before us. Whether it was regarding being kind to each other, respecting our elders, or learning important life lessons such as the value of being clean, my parents could rest assured that their family rules of conduct were upheld when they were absent.

Just because we're poor doesn't mean we are nasty! my mother would tell us. The translation was, "Just because we don't have all the money we need, does not mean the Grahams can't keep themselves clean, presentable, and respectable."

Sweet old Miss Mel. Although she was the source of many whippings on my behind, I have to thank her for not only the discipline reminders she delivered, but I will be eternally grateful for one major contribution she planted into my life journey. Because there were so many mouths to feed and new babies that needed attention, we often went without the simple things. In my case, I had never had a birthday party. On my seventh birthday, Miss Mel put together a long table made of cinder blocks and boards so my siblings and the neighborhood kids and I could sit on each side of the table and enjoy a birthday celebration. Clean white bed sheets served as tablecloths. Candy, cups of Kool-Aid, and a beautiful birthday cake baked in my honor made quite an impression on me.

I was bursting with pride as I looked around the table and realized the trouble someone had gone to, just to celebrate my birthday! Kids need to know that they matter to someone. I knew my family loved me, but to have someone outside the family—especially, the woman for whom I had caused such grief—throw a celebration for me was an act of kindness I have never forgotten. But, there was more. When the cake, Kool-Aid, and candies were consumed, Miss Mel revealed one more surprise.

"Happy birthday, Charles," Miss Mel said as she handed me a wrapped gift. "Go ahead. Open it."

My eyes must have been as big as silver dollars as I received the gift from her hands. The party guests were on the edges of their seats to see what was under the wrapping paper.

"I figured you'd like it."

I stared at my first "paint-by-numbers" paint set. Miss Mel had "figured" correctly. I didn't just like it; I loved it. More importantly, it demonstrated in the simplest way that someone can support someone else just by taking a real interest in them. Miss Mel did not have to do anything for me that day. She could have given me a simple Happy Birthday greeting and been done with it. But instead, she gave me my first birthday party and perhaps my most memorable gift. I loved to be creative. I wanted to learn to draw and paint, and she was observant enough to grasp that dream she saw in me.

When I put everything into context and realize the significant role she played in the life of all the Graham children and the support she daily gave to my parents and all the families in the community, I realize the tremendous value she was in our lives. Today, many persons don't even know the name of the neighbor living a few feet away from them. We had the high privilege of a grandmotherly female influence watching over our welfare at no charge to my mom and dad. I would go so far as to say it was her "calling" in life. She understood it, and she accepted her calling without question.

CHAPTER 7

"The Influence of Mom and Dad"

Miss Melvina and our neighbors had strong influences on my daily life, but nothing could take the place of having a loving mother and father like mine, nurturing me and impacting my character, my emotions, and my decisions. I loved having Mother in the house. When she was away, there was always a piece missing.

The trouble for me started with one of her announcements:

"I got a job as a cook," Mother informed us.

Mother started working out of the house in order to earn money to feed and clothe us, and she began devoting much of her life to other families. As a teenager, I resented the injustice to our family, and her working for others churned up the feelings of injustice in me. She was my mother, not someone else's! She was meant to be in our home when I woke up in the morning. She was supposed to tend to her children and me, not someone else's children. I hated the fact that Mother was suddenly at the beck and call of another child and his or her needs. She wasn't supposed to be across town with some other kid and his family. She was supposed to be nearby for my hurts and my needs, not the needs of people who had her in their home for convenience. It started to get to me. I had endured enough of her absence.

"Where are you gonna be a cook, Mother?"

"I'll be cooking for a Mrs. Mary Ruth across town."

We all knew what that meant. She was cooking for a family on the other side of town. I knew she was happy to have another income to add to the Grahams' bottom line, but it didn't make me happy.

My mother was a school cafeteria cook, a cook for a white family across town, and a cook and mother for the Grahams. The workload that my sweet mother had to bear was too much. The net result for my siblings and me was less Momma time. When we did get time with her, she was often exhausted from expending all her best energy somewhere else.

One day, I took it upon myself to fix the situation. You see, every significant holiday that came around, the tradition for us was that my mother was expected to be cooking for and serving the white family. My frustration reached a boiling point when Mother announced again that she wouldn't be spending Thanksgiving with us, but she'd be cooking and serving the white family across town. I wasn't a little child anymore the day I showed up at the door of her employer.

"My Mom won't be cooking for you anymore," I told the woman of the house.

To say the least, she was surprised to see me and even more startled to hear the message I just delivered.

"My mother will not be coming back."

With that abrupt announcement, the deed was done. I did not care what might happen after that. I only knew that I was going to bat for my dear mother, who was working her fingers to the bone. Even if she received appreciation from the white family who hired her to do all their domestic service, the fact was, Mother had lots of children who had endured years of her absence so she could serve others.

I can't tell you the sense of satisfaction I got when the holiday meal was placed on the table. Everyone was full of smiles and gratitude as Mother's chair was occupied for the first time in a long time. The look on her face was priceless. Oh, and by the way, despite my taking Mother away for the holiday, the family would not let Mom go. They asked her to stay on her job with them because they did not want to lose her.

In these modern times, it is so difficult to be a stay-at-home parent. Women and men would love to stay at home and pour their wisdom and kindness into their kids, but often it simply is not practical or affordable. I truly consider myself a very blessed man because I had a wonderful, strong, and caring spiritual mother raising my siblings and me. In Proverbs, King Solomon says that we, as children, should obey the commands of our father and learn from the teachings of our mother. Mom was a true teacher in my life.

I recall many instances in my home when Mom would take the time to apply life lessons in front of me so I could be equipped for the future. She would say things such as:

You can't just go out and spend money you don't have.

Mother was a stickler on living within her means, and she made it abundantly clear that we should do the same. She taught us how to budget money, for one thing. She would lay the money out on the kitchen table and ask Joyce to count it out. She would make a list of all the items she needed for the home. Whether it was the grocery store, the furniture store, or the hardware store, Momma had the transaction figured to the penny before she truly considered her purchase.

"If you don't have it, you don't spend it," she told us in no uncertain terms.

"Yes, ma'am."

"Pick up your pencil and write this down."

"Yes, ma'am."

"Wells Grocery; twenty-five. Western Auto; nine. Abrams; twelve-fifty."

Mom read her list with conviction.

Joyce quickly wrote down whatever Mother said.

"How much is that?"

"Ummm, forty-six-dollars and fifty cents."

If Mother sat silent for a moment that typically meant that the figure she just heard was unworkable.

"I have forty dollars."

"Yes, ma'am," Joyce and Wanda nodded.

Mother picked up her list and began to adjust what she would pay that month. As soon as she got everything subtracted and added back in, my sister and I would wait patiently. Joyce carefully added each item and made her calculations. When it came even to the penny, our work was done, and a trip to town was planned.

That's how things worked financially in the Graham house. Mother's diligence was much more instructive than any math or personal finance class I was required to take in high school or college. It was real-world logic using absolutes of money.

"If we don't have it, we don't spend it" was a creed to live by.

A few years ago, I invited some of my mother's life-long friends to a birthday party I was hosting for her. Dozens of family members and friends showed up for the cake and ice cream. They wanted to show their love and respect to a woman who had made such an impact on all of us.

"Your mother never owed me money," a local banker said as he shook my hand. "Ollie Graham was very particular in paying her debts."

Obviously, he was telling me in order to compliment her and honor her as a woman of trustworthiness.

"Yes, sir. She taught us all well," I assured him.

There is a proverb that says that we should listen to the teachings of our mothers. There is also a commandment that tells me to honor my mother and father. It is the only commandment of the ten that has a promise connected to it.

Besides her locally famous cooking skills, we definitely knew our mother as the cleanest person we or anyone else had ever seen.

One day I asked a family friend, Mrs. Bernice Jackson, "What do you remember about my mom when we were living in Boydell?"

"Your mother was the cleanest person I knew."

The most public example was my mother's detail while doing the laundry. I say "public" because after the drudgery of hand washing, her clean laundry would make it to the clothesline to be on display for the public to see. Mother's process was to be adhered to, no matter what. Washday was almost every other day, and Henry Ford himself would have been impressed by the assembly line-like coordination that my mother instituted.

First, a fire was built under a large cast iron pot. Secondly, the clothing was rubbed violently up and down a scrub board or a washboard in order to force the dirt free from the cloth. Thirdly, the white clothes were always boiled for optimum soil removal. The total process was: fire, scrub, rinse, boil whites, rinse. I can still hear the rubbing and rinsing in my mind.

The clean clothes were hung on the line; but not just any line-hanging method would do. Each article of clothing had a position on the line. Every similar piece of clothing lived together as they dried in the sun. Shirts, pants, towels, or whatever had its exact placement. Mother even had a method for the removal of the clothing from the clothesline. It was designed not only for the ease of taking down the clothes and folding, but it also led to the order of the ironing of the clothes. Every type of clothing made its way together through the routine.

It's difficult for me to describe the sheer intricacy and perfection of Mother's clothesline. When she had everything pinned to the line, the collection of cloth and color became almost a piece of art. It wasn't just the neighborhood that knew her clothesline was art flowing in the breeze, one day a man stopped to photograph Mom's laundry moving gracefully against the Arkansas sky.

My dad was a practical man. His needs were simple, which was a good thing, because he had to learn to function as a husband and a father while earning very little money. When I think of my father, I remember him being a hard worker who was dependable and competent. Dad could operate anything on the farm, which made him invaluable to the owner. He was also a no-nonsense man with firm expectations and he had no patience for our misbehavior.

Dad was a humble man. When you don't have a lot of material possessions, and every day is a struggle, life has a way of humbling you, and when you're raised poor, there is a very fine line that separates humility from being humiliated. Take my dad's car, for instance. My dad's cars always had problems—lots of problems.

It reminds me of the little boy who asked his mother, *Mom, what happens to old cars?*

They sell them to your dad, the mother tells him.

When you don't have the money to keep a car maintained, you learn to live with whatever attributes the car is willing to give back as it ages and succumbs to rust and wear. My most vivid car memories as a child are regarding the times that Dad's old car would function in all the important ways … except starting.

"We saw you all pushing your dad's car today!" the kids would say as they laughed.

When a family has money for car repairs, they don't usually have to get out and push their vehicle like we had to.

"Get out of the car!" Dad would shout.

All of us kids knew what that meant. Sometimes it was because the car wouldn't start, or the car was out of fuel, or the car's engine had given out. Sometimes we were ordered out of the car to keep something bad from happening. When Dad had reached the railroad tracks on the way to or from our house, we all had to bail out as if we were performing a fire drill. If Dad attempted to cross the tracks with our family weighing the car down, the exhaust pipe had been known to fall off, and the old heap could then be heard for miles. Believe me; I know. It happened too many times.

I heard one boy say, "If the city wants to spray for mosquitoes, all they have to do is call your dad and have him drive around town."

Yes, it was harsh and it was rude, but it was a creative way of saying that my dad's car was well known for its blue cloud of smoke that hung all over Dermott after he passed through.

We moved from Boydell to what was called "Skipper Bridge." The actual bridge for which the area is named provided even more adventure. You don't find bridges in the United States like these much anymore, thank goodness. Skipper Bridge was a one-lane bridge without guardrails, and in order to safely cross the bridge, a person had to align their car tires on two rows of raised wooden planks that ran along the top of the bridge's surface.

Mother did not always trust my dad to safely navigate the bridge with all her precious cargo inside. I can remember that it would really upset Dad that Mom had evacuated the car of all us kids. Once the family was safely across and waiting on the other side, Dad would accelerate the engine and swiftly cross the bridge with the skill of a Hollywood stunt driver, much to the chagrin of my mother. My brothers all thought it was pretty awesome.

But before he would do that stunt, my brothers and sisters would dash across the planks of the bridge and reach the other side, leaving me standing next to the car, frozen in place. I mentioned that I was deathly afraid of water.

"Come on, Charles," the guys jeered as I got on all fours and crawled across the wooden planks.

Oh, how I hated crossing that bridge! In fact, there were times when Dad and Mom were going to town that I just quickly volunteered to babysit, or I'd pretend to be ill in order to avoid another crawl across Skipper Bridge.

Dad's influence was a major part of what made me the man I am today. He taught me life lessons that have endured time and change as the years passed. Yes, he was a strict disciplinarian, but in retrospect I see clearly that he wanted to raise me to understand honesty and good character. He did have a loving side that came to the surface on special occasions.

At Christmastime, my dad and mother created a Graham family tradition that sticks in my mind. Each season they would make it a point to purchase oranges and apples for us. When my brothers and sisters and I were out of the house, they would carefully hide the delicious fruit, hopefully preserving the treats to be used as Christmas gifts.

Dad would step on a chair and tuck the boxes safely away in the rafters. I'm sure that Mom and he assumed that they were out of sight and out of reach. The part they did not take into consideration was the smelling ability of hungry kids. The temptation for my sisters and brothers and me was just too much. After Dad placed the fruit in the rafters, the unmistakable smell of fresh apples and oranges easily permeating our little home.

One winter day, when Mom and Dad were gone, we searched for the fruit, following the wonderful scent. We were ecstatic to find the hidden treasure. We were smart enough to use some ingenuity and self-discipline in order to have a quick taste but not get caught. One of us would sneak an apple or an orange out of the box and share slices equally. We thought our caution and sneakiness paid off because as far as we knew, our parents never caught on.

Dad and Mom made sure that "sharing" was always a part of our vocabulary and part of our character.

"Share with your brother. Share with your sister."

Those were two phrases I heard all through my childhood. The Christmas season was no different. When one of us got a toy, it was understood by all of us that at some point we had to let our brothers and sisters play with the item.

One year, my brother Stanley and I got a bicycle. One can immediately see what's wrong with that situation. Two young boys on the edge of their emotions and filled with excitement are told that the bicycle they got for Christmas is theirs to share. Stanley did not like sharing, and I didn't like sharing. Although two negatives are supposed to make a positive, all the math calculations in the world were not going to add up to our getting along with one bicycle. Not only did Stanley wish to dominate the riding of our bike, his friends showed up and wanted him to ride along with them. His friends all had their own bicycles, and his buddies made it clear that they did not want me to ride along. They just wanted Stanley. Because we had to take turns, his friends would only ride when Stanley rode. When I rode the bike, I rode alone. When I gave the bike back to Stanley, his friends would join him again.

During one of the rides, Stanley and his friend decided to blaze on past me with the intention of keeping possession of the bicycle and riding it for the rest of the evening. As they approached, their intention was to speed up and zip past me. I knew exactly what they were up to, so when they got close, I quickly grabbed the handlebar, which threw poor Stanley off the bike and onto the gravel road, where he hit headfirst. In one moment, Stanley went from having fun on our bike to suffering an injury and bleeding badly from the gash on his forehead.

It was one of those moments you have as a kid where you suddenly get the notion; *I did not see that coming!* Stanley got to his feet and discovered the blood oozing from the wound. In a split second he was dashing to Mother, who was outside doing laundry, to show her and tell her what I had done.

"Momma! Charles made me wreck," Stanley whimpered.

That's all Mother had to hear. She grabbed an electrical cord that was connected to her old washing machine that sat in the yard.

"Charles!" Mother shouted. "If you run, I'll kill you!"

I froze for a moment and had to make a split-second decision. Should I stay and take the beating, or should I run and somehow delay the beating? Seeing the extension cord clutched in her hand left me no choice. I decided to run as fast as I could run. Like Forrest Gump, I prepared myself to keep running from village to village. I was prepared to do what I had to do to avoid the wrath of my mother. Before I knew it, I heard the patter of the multiple sneakers of all Stanley's buddies coming in my direction. This was it; run harder and faster or get the beating of my life. You see, in our neighborhood, anytime a kid ran by and he was being chased, everyone joined the chase. It was an instant posse that formed to capture the runner.

"Gotcha," one of Stanley's buddies said as he grabbed me.

The rest of the boys quickly grabbed, tugged and pulled on me as if I were an escaped convict who had broken out of maximum security. At that moment I think I would have gladly taken a high security prison with solitary confinement. At least I would have been protected from the impending spanking. Whip me she did.

My life lesson from that unforgettable incident was to share. Had I understood that lesson earlier, I could have avoided having to learn at the end of an extension cord.

Dad and Mother continued to teach me right and wrong until I was old enough to make my own decisions. I can't thank them enough for their influence on how I make decisions today.

I love my mother. From my earliest memories as a child to this day, my mother has been and continues to be a profound influence on my life. Since moving back to Dermott, her life and our relationship have continued to shape who I am as a man. Helping her with her daily care and needs, I have had to reach deep within myself to develop even more patience and understanding of what my role is in her life. With the gift of hindsight, I can now look back on my younger years and understand that my mother was always doing the best she could with the limited resources that she had.

CHAPTER 8

"Crowded House"

My house at Baxter was packed with a ton of kids and two adults, and the word "privacy" was unheard of. The old house had four rooms plus a storage room. As we walked through the boys' room on our way to the porch, we would pass a small storage area that one-day I determined would be christened "Charles' room." Anyone who really knows me understands that I like having a space that I call my own. Having a bunch of other siblings impacting my privacy was not how I wanted to live as a young teen. With some verbal persuasion I tried to convince Momma to allow me to lay claim to the storage room and make it my own.

"I'll decorate it. I'll paint it. I'll arrange it real nice, and it will be the best room in the house. Please, Momma, I'm going crazy without my own space," I pleaded.

Mother gave in, and the process of design and decoration was on. The room would be my room, and although the other kids might interpret the gesture, as a bit of favoritism, they knew that I would turn the drab, underutilized storage space into a room I could be proud of.

My first piece of furniture was a cot that served as my bed. More importantly, it meant that for the first time in my life I would be sleeping by myself! I then gathered the savings I had accumulated from picking cotton and made my way to Morgan and Lindsay, a department store in town that had most everything I would need. Keep in mind that this time of my teen years would have been around 1970 when the United States was having a real transition in decor and fashion. We had moved out of the bell-bottoms and medallions around our neck and moved into the pointed-collared nylon shirts and platform shoes. There was still way too much velvet art going on, but some fashion and art statements die a slow death.

"This is it!" I exclaimed as I saw a royal blue crushed velvet bedspread.

"Excellent choice," Mrs. Burchfield replied. "And, that bedspread comes with matching curtains."

"You're kidding! I'll take them too," I told her with confidence.

After the cot was covered in velvet and the curtains were hung on the window, my brothers and sisters were as thrilled as I. They wholeheartedly approved.

"This is the best thing ever, Charles!"

"I love this room."

"I want to live in here with you, Charles."

My siblings couldn't wait to tell all the kids in our farm community about what their brother had done.

"You gotta come see Charles' room!"

"Charles got a new room, and he's decorated it really nice."

Before long I felt like a tour guide in my bedroom. My room wasn't just the talk of the immediate family; my room was the talk of the whole neighborhood.

"Look at that! Everything matches so perfectly."

"It's like a department store in here!"

Kids were in awe of my work, and I must admit that my head was swelling quite a bit from the praise. However, once the initial compliments calmed down, and kids had experienced the tour of my room, I had to lay down the law that my room was just that: MY ROOM. No one was allowed to enter my space without the consent of the owner and master of the domain, Charles Graham.

My little oasis brought a measure of peace to my home life. It was off limits to everyone but me, and so it became my personal getaway space. I would lie on my bed and dream of how it would be one day when I owned my own house and my own things would surround me.

As I lay there on my bed, I thought of the cars and trucks I heard passing by on the two-lane highway, and I imagined where those people must have been going. There was a bigger and better world out there, where I could spread my wings and make something of myself. But how could I do it? When would I do it? I was simply Charles Graham from Dermott, Arkansas. Most everyone I knew had grown up in Dermott, choosing to stay in the area to do what their father or mother did before them.

Somehow, my own space provided that incubator I needed to hold my dreams and let them form in my mind. I cherished my wonderful room. Every detail was my personal expression of who I was and who I wanted to be. People who came to visit saw my creation, and when they praised me for it, I loved the warm feeling that affirmation gave me. People commenting on my talents made me feel even more as if I didn't fit in where we lived. I felt out of place, and I felt that God must have a special plan that was very different from living on a farm and picking cotton.

Even the things hanging from my ceiling were touches of art from my imagination. My entire room was transformed into a special place wherein I could express my art. I always enjoyed painting and creating things, and my space afforded me the silence and elbowroom to develop one thing after another.

One creative day, I took a favorite sweatshirt and sliced the sleeves in a vertical fashion to give it some Charles Graham style. I then designed a peace sign and black power sign to adorn the back of the sweatshirt. Wow, it was a bold statement. It wasn't a political statement. It was just a statement that I wanted to march to a different beat. I was creative, confident, and determined to make my way in the world. My pride for that one-of-a-kind sweatshirt hanging in my uniquely decorated room was torn apart one day. And when I say *torn apart,* I mean it literally.

The new serenity and escape in my personal space was invaded by a sibling dispute of epic proportions. My side of the story goes like this: my younger sister and I were left to babysit the little ones. Honestly, I can't remember exactly the nature of the argument, but I think that Wanda and I said we were going to be famous by being acrobats in the circus. We had perfected a routine whereby I would lie on the floor on my back. She would sit on my feet, and I would thrust her forward as if she were shot from a cannon. I think that's how it started. One day, while practicing for our debut in the circus, I thrust her a little too far, slamming her into the wall. Once she pulled herself to her feet and regained her composure, she turned to me and shouted,

"You did that on purpose!"

"I did not!" I tried to assure her.

The sibling spat gradually escalated into a brother-and-sister fight to end all sibling battles. Wanda and I yelled, and we screamed, and then we yelled some more. We shouted back and forth at each other until the verbal battle had nowhere else to go but to the ripping and shredding of personal property! As the fight reached its boiling point, the gloves came off, and Wanda did the one thing that should have never been done. She stormed toward my new room.

"Oh, no you don't! Don't you go in my room!"

"You're not going to stop me!"

"Wanda!" I shouted. "Don't do it!"

Wanda was on fire with rage when she blew past me and burst into my room. First, she went to the thing that she knew would inflict immediate pain. She grabbed my original design, black power sweatshirt and began ripping it to shreds.

"You like ripped sweat shirts? I'll help you rip it some more!"

"Wanda, I'm gonna kill you!"

So much for the peace sign on the front of my sweatshirt. Peace in the Graham house was shattered that moment as Wanda continued screaming and ripping my sweatshirt.

That began the mutual destruction of each other's personal property.

"You're crazy!"

"It's stupid-looking anyway!"

"You're stupid!"

I turned and stomped into the girls' room.

"Oh, no you don't! Get outta there!" Wanda screamed.

Hanging on the wall was a delicate three-dimensional poster of the solar system that I had helped Wanda make for her science class.

"You tore up something of mine!"

"You wouldn't dare!"

"It's what you get."

"Don't you do it, Charles."

Wanda's protesting was no match for my rage. Like Darth Vader and the storm troopers, I went after the 3-D poster board solar system, and it didn't have a chance.

She had shredded and destroyed my sweatshirt beyond repair, and it was time for Wanda's solar system to die. I grabbed the sun and its planets and ripped them apart as Wanda watched. Rip, rip, rip! In three seconds the universe was history.

Joyce, our sister the peacemaker, ran into the room.

"Stop it! Stop!" she said as she picked up the pieces from the floor.

"Mom and Dad will kill us all! Please, stop it!"

Joyce was right. Our parents didn't like it at all when any of us got rowdy in the house. The whippings wouldn't end with just Wanda and me, but every one of the older kids would be in danger of some punishment as well. We knew that because it would not be the first time everyone would get a whipping because of someone else breaking the rules. The problem with Joyce's plea to stop was the simple fact that Wanda and I had some more fighting left in us, and we weren't ready to listen to common sense.

I dashed back into my room, and I pushed a chest of drawers into the doorway to try to fortify my room.

"Stay out of my room, Wanda!"

"Why did you tear up my solar system?"

"You deserved it."

"I did not."

"Did too. Stay out!"

Before I could react, Wanda did her best ninja imitation as she slid under the chest and stood up in my room.

"This ain't over."

"Get out!"

Joyce came to the doorway, holding bits and pieces of the paper universe.

"I told you Momma's gonna kill us all!"

The only way I can explain what happened next is that our rage pushed us completely to a point of irrational thinking. We didn't take time to consider the certain consequences we would suffer when our parents returned. Pure, red-hot revenge was driving the both of us. After almost every personal item that each of us possessed was thrown, stomped on, and damaged beyond repair, the infamous "Battle of Charles and Wanda" came to a quiet halt.

Wanda was shaking and breathing hard. I was panting and sweating. We stood staring at each other as if we were looking at a stranger.

Finally, Joyce broke the silence:

"We're dead."

Fortunately, the Grahams have a tradition of making up quickly. We caught our breath, and our good sense returned.

"I'm sorry, Charles," Wanda said.

"I'm sorry I tore up your solar system, Wanda," I replied.

Our love for each other overcame the temporary anger. I have always been close to my sisters Wanda, Joyce, and Grace, and there was no way I could stay mad at Wanda, no matter what had happened. Plus, we knew that Mom and Dad would whip the tar out of us if they ever found out what happened. We committed ourselves to a peace treaty, as well as an agreement and promise that under no circumstances would we tell on each other. Wanda's art was destroyed, and I would never wear my favorite sweatshirt again, but love was restored, and life was back to normal before Mom and Dad got home.

I'll wrap up this chapter by simply saying that when you survive crowded communal living as I did during my childhood, memories are filled with many stories of just trying to make it through. Allow me to give you some examples:

When one or more of us got sick, we were required to take castor oil mixed with sugar ... as if sugar would disguise that nasty taste! Living in such tight quarters meant it was even more important to get the sick kid well. There were lots of home remedies such as Pepto Bismol mixed with flour and warm pepper. Honestly, some of Mom's concoctions were so horrible that we only got sick once! So in that respect her homemade medicines were very effective.

During the cold and flu seasons, we could always count on Momma coming into our rooms and generously lathering our chests with Vicks VapoRub. She would spread it on us thick as if she were frosting a cake. There was so much menthol in the air we could barely open our eyes. Speaking of eyes, if we ever got any of that medicine in our eyes, it made the other parts of being sick seem just fine! Wow, it burned.

Mother also forced us to take another one of her secret mixtures of unhappiness when she thought we needed to regurgitate something from a sour stomach. A little bit of sugar, turpentine, and some bitter yellow stuff did the trick.

Mother's list for curing whatever ailed her kids read like a laundry list of old fashion remedies. If a wasp stung us, a saliva-covered piece of chewing tobacco applied to the sting did the trick. If we had a toothache, Mother boiled some kind of root and made tea for us to drink.

The legendary healing protocol that may have literally saved my life happened when I was about five years old, when I was struck with violent childhood seizures. My body was almost lifeless when my Aunt Bertha and Uncle L.C. arrived and anointed me with oil. They gathered large green leaves and proceeded to cover my body from my neck to my toes. Once the leaves were placed on my skin, Mother and Aunt Bertha wrapped my little body in a shroud made of a white bed sheets. Uncle L.C. and Aunt Bertha, who were pastors, then prayed for me. Sometime during my parents' sleepless and prayer-filled night, my deadly fever broke. The leaves and tightly wrapped sheet on me had drawn much of the toxicity from my pores. I was healed by their miracle cure and by the prayers prayed for me.

My last home remedy was definitely not one that my mother or Aunt and Uncle dreamed up. On one occasion, while Mother was still at work, Joyce conjured up her own home remedy. It was concocted after she got a simple cut on her foot while "hooking" beans. She was using a long hooked knife to weed the beans and accidentally cut herself.

"Momma's gonna be really mad when she sees what I did."

"How're you going to hide a bleeding cut?" we asked.

"I'm gonna pack it with dirt."

"What? That ain't gonna work."

"You watch. I'll pack dirt in there, and Momma will never know it even happened."

Well, Mother discovered what Joyce had done while giving her a bath that night. Her wound got infected. I can't recall the punishment Joyce received for playing the role of doctor, but the result was her missing three and a half days of classes and having to wear humiliating house shoes to school for a while.

It was a blessing to grow up in such a crowded house. I used to lie in my cot and find myself asking God questions such as: *If You really knew all about me, even before I was made, why was I born into these conditions?*

But as I look back on those times full of trials and fussing and debating every little thing, I seriously wouldn't trade it now for anything. Yes, when I say we were a "close family," it does have a double meaning. However, it was that crowded environment that taught me how to love a little more, tolerate a lot more, and appreciate so much more where God has brought me to this day.

CHAPTER 9

"Church"

The Grahams were and still are church people. It's our way of life. Hearing adults talk about spiritual things was in no way foreign to me as a child. Being in the church house was simply what we did with one or more days of our week. Spending quality time in church was something we loved to do, and looking back, I realize it helped solidify my relationships with my brothers and sisters.

This chapter of my story, I'm going to attempt to paint a clear and vibrant picture of how my spiritual life and church life began. Going to Evergreen Missionary Baptist Church in Boydell on Sundays was a welcomed break from the Monday-to-Saturday routine of families working in the fields. On Saturday night, one of my dad's many rituals was to clean each and every child's shoes for Sunday morning. Monday through Saturday night, our poor shoes would be put through the grind due to hard work, walking to school, and running down the dirt roads. By the time my dad got to the end of cleaning off the caked-on mud from all the many shoes, I'm sure he was sick of the chore, but he never let on. It was an act of fatherly love for his kids, and as I grew older, I realized it was also an example set for my family and me that we were to dress up and appear in the Father's house looking our best. It was a way to honor the sanctity of being in God's house.

Going to church was all about developing my faith. Faith is a wonderful word that was and still is the cornerstone principle of my life. The necessity of a lifestyle of faith was introduced to me from day one. I was born into a family where faith wasn't just a concept that was talked about, but it was on a daily display. My mother and father had faith to trust that God would help them feed, clothe, and raise their large family.

When I was born, my parents were members of Evergreen Missionary Baptist Church in Boydell, Arkansas. My mother is still a member of the church, and I enjoy attending with her and ministering there on occasion. Imagine a wooden building sitting on the edge of a field next to Bayou Bartholomew. An old cemetery sits on the church grounds, as does the old outhouse that I was afraid to use when I was a boy. The outside of the church is made of wood and painted white. Inside, the church has wooden plank floors and walls.

One day a week we attended church and got to see our hardworking neighbors and friends in a much different light. Dads that we normally saw in blue jeans and maybe an old flannel shirt were dressed in suits, button-up white shirts, colorful neckties, and various kinds of felt hats. Ladies that I saw working in the fields would show up for church dressed from head to toe in beautiful dresses, hats, and high-heeled shoes. After church services, I used to count the holes left in the ground by the women's high-heeled shoes. The prim and proper ladies' heels would nearly sink in the soft ground. Although walking was a challenge in the spongy soil, those proud women would step across the lawn as if they were strolling along a New York City sidewalk.

The steadfast members of Evergreen Missionary Baptist Church could always be found in their same places in the pews. Someone had to be deathly ill or worse (such as passed on) to not be found sitting in his or her usual seat. Like a well-trained military brigade, all the members had their roles and their positions in the church. Our members were faithful, loving, and committed to being the Church in action. However, if someone accidentally or purposely imposed upon someone else's place on the pews, the atmosphere would change. For example, if our sweet little ladies discovered their normal places in the pews encroached upon, some of their sweetness could sour, and they would make it clear that they were upset about it.

When I say they had their position in the church, I mean they had their role to play. For example, our revered church ushers were self-appointed police. They were the enforcers who demanded reverence in the House of God. It was expected that kids were to mind their manners and show respect while in the church. There were some of us who thought it would be fun to etch our names in the old wooden pews. That was definitely a punishable offense. If the ushers ever caught us, we would pay for it by receiving a tongue-lashing. Then, our parents were notified.

Other punishable offenses were fanning ourselves too aggressively with the paper fans or chewing gum and sticking it under the pews. If we were disrupting the order of the service in any way, an usher was there to tell us to settle down and remember where we were. The sanctuary and the service were to be held in the highest esteem and paid the utmost respect.

The podium where the preacher delivered his messages was especially holy. After the service, if an adult saw a child getting near the pulpit, he or she would shout out, *Get that child,* as if the child might drop dead going onto the pulpit area. It was "holy ground."

The reverence wasn't just for the podium, but it was for the church as a whole. We admittedly broke lots of rules, and it is fun going back to the old church these days to see my childhood friends' names permanently scratched into the wood.

If you have ever had the joy of attending a lively church where men and women "get happy," you know exactly what I mean. The pastor would work his way through the powerful sermon that God had given him and as the Spirit rose up within him, certain members would be energized right along with him!

The ushers with church fans in hand stood ready to help those who were getting happier and happier as the Spirit moved among the pews. Their "fanning" job was to flutter those fans as fast as they could to move the air in order to calm the dear souls who were overflowing with happiness.

Often, a little ninety-pound lady would begin to shout, jerk, and quake to the point where it would take two or three grown men to subdue her. The designated men would grab a flailing arm or leg and carry the energized soul down the aisle and right out the door.

One sweet lady, Miss Lena, comes to mind. She loved Jesus as much as any person could. As the Holy Spirit rose in her on Sunday morning, she began to help out the preacher with a shout; then another and another followed until she was completely overcome with the presence of the Lord. It was Miss Lena's character to "fall out" into the aisle in front of God and everyone.

It was amazing to me that ladies could fall out so dramatically and still maintain such composure in regards to their fashion. Purses were neatly clutched under one arm, dresses stayed tucked under, and wigs never shifted or fell off. "Getting happy" moments were filled with grace and control.

There was another important role that several of our men accepted. They had the distinct position of protecting the preacher if things got out of control. Believe it or not, there were women who would quake, shout, and then run up and slap the preacher on the back or shoulder. You read that correctly; they would slap the pastor. The pastors counted on the deacons to run interference for protection.

Despite the dedication and willingness of our deacons to throw their bodies in front of the man of God, we did have one particular preacher who would take matters into his own hands and take off running. He had the "every-man-for-himself" approach. I got the sneaking suspicion that he had been slapped one too many times during his preaching.

One day I got dressed in my Sunday best, but it wasn't for our regular church service. I was attending my first funeral. I remember it very well as my family and I gathered to pay our final respects to my Uncle "Kinsey," the husband of my mom's sister. His given name was actually "McKinley Reese." I was pretty young, and for the longest time some of the words spoken at that funeral had me confused. The preacher kept looking at my poor aunt and the grieving family and saying, "Our prayers go out to the 'Be-Reese' family."

The preacher would nod and offer his most sympathetic look to the family.

"When we leave here today, don't forget to keep the 'Be-Reese' family in your prayers," he reminded us.

Every funeral I attended from that point on, I couldn't figure out how the deceased seemed to always be related to me. Preachers would constantly mention the Be-Reese family. It took a while, but I later learned that the preacher was referring to the bereaved family, not the Be-Reese family.

My first attempted official entrance into the church family was when I was five years old. During a spirited revival, God convicted me, and I knew I had to ask Jesus into my heart and become a follower of Him. I can remember to this day the excitement that filled me, knowing that I was a child of God. However, much of the emotional excitement quickly dissipated. When I got home my big brother, Curtis, filled me in as to the details of my upcoming baptism.

"The preacher's gonna baptize you where Mr. Levi catches them big gars! That gar's gonna bite your face off!" Curtis teased.

Mr. Levi was one of Dad's friends who set trotlines in the bayou in order to catch fish. I may have been young, but I knew what a gar was. It was a long fish with sharp teeth—a bottom-dweller that lived in the murky waters of the bayou. Just picture a long-bodied fish with an angry alligator mouth. Most garfish will be about twenty inches in length, but if they are allowed to grow in the wild, some gars may grow up to nine feet long and can weigh several hundred pounds. I can assure you that when my brother said I was going to be baptized where Mr. Levi caught gars, in my mind the gars suddenly grew to the size of a dinosaur!

I knew I loved Jesus, but I also knew that I hated gars. So something was going to have to give. It was bad enough that I was deathly afraid of water, but picturing a monster fish in that dark water with me was more than I could bear. Whenever I saw Mr. Levi in church, I would sit as far away from him as possible, just in case he had one of those baby varmints in his pocket. A five-year-old with a vivid imagination cannot be too careful.

As my baptismal day got closer, the teasing from my brothers got worse.

"On Sunday morning when you're dunked under water, that big ole gar is gonna bite your face off, Charles!"

"Be quiet!"

"He's gonna git you and eat you up!"

I could picture those sharp gar teeth coming at my face once my head was under the murky brown water. Fatal images of my impending baptism haunted me for the rest of the revival. I certainly didn't regret asking Jesus into my heart, but I definitely had regrets about being signed up for baptism!

Sunday morning came, and my heart was about to explode with fear. Meanwhile, most of my family and extended family gathered. They were proud that I was following our Lord in baptism. My grandmother made a white baptismal gown for me.

I trembled with fear from head to toe as the entire congregation and about twenty other baptismal candidates and I marched from the church to the unforgiving waters of the bayou. On this fateful day, I was about the twelfth "victim" in line, as I saw it.

As the baptismal party stood in line on the shore, the deacons assisted each candidate down the bank. The pastor in the bayou waited patiently to administer our dunking. I stood in line as instructed, but as my turn came and the deacon reached for me, I would jump behind the kid following me. I hoped it looked as though I was simply being polite, but thinking back, I'm sure everyone could see in my body language that I was scared stiff as I postponed the inevitable.

You would think that my siblings would have given me support by the time I was in the line of obedient servants of God who were publicly professing their faith in Jesus. But as I looked over to my brothers, all I could see was my big brother clasping his hands together, imitating a gar sinking its teeth into me. Thump, thump, thump, went my heart. I thought it would beat right out of my chest.

It was my turn. I tried to slip behind another candidate, but my dad glared and mouthed the words, "Stop that."

I was as scared as I had ever been during my five short years of life. The deacons must have realized that when they reached for me. As they approached, I reached down, girded up my loins, and took off running for home as fast as my little feet could take me. Dad and my siblings could only watch as I disappeared down the road toward our house.

When I made it to the house, my mother, who was very pregnant and unable to attend the baptism, looked at me with surprise. I was breathing hard, and I was as dry as a bone. She knew that there was no way I had been baptized. A few years later as she would tell the story she would say:

"I knew he had not been baptized because he came back home just as dry as he left."

It took about five years, but I finally worked up the courage to enter the bayou's mysterious waters. I needed all the courage I could gather because although I had overcome the fear of a gar eating me, I hadn't overcome my inability to swim. As I was led out into the water by one of the deacons, I began to feel as if I couldn't breathe. The higher the water came upon me, the less breath I seemed to catch. People who don't fear water—those who learned to swim and enjoy being submerged—don't understand the paralyzing fear that people like me feel. I began to hyperventilate as the water reached my chest. When I stopped wading out, I could only gasp for air. My body was shaking and quaking as the preacher began to preach. I'm sure our preacher could see that he had to make this event happen quickly or he would be baptizing a body that would be limp and unconscious.

There I was, trying desperately to catch my breath, and the minister was finding all kinds of things to say about getting saved and baptized. One of my aunts somehow confused my shaking and quaking as some sort of extra filling of the Spirit, and that made her shout for joy.

"Jesus, Jesus, Jesus!" Aunt Nancy shouted.

Because of Aunt Nancy's excitement, the preacher felt inspired to preach. Eventually, he got to the task at hand, and I was thrust under. Unfortunately, I forgot to take that last good breath before I was submerged. When I was "resurrected to new life," I came out of that water with a portion of the bayou in my mouth and one thing on my mind; get back to land!

At age ten, I was a full-fledged, baptized Christian believer in our active church. I can only describe the atmosphere in our little Friendship Baptist Church in Baxter, Arkansas, as something out of a Hollywood movie. We entered the sanctuary, where rows of wooden pews faced the pulpit.

On a small stage at the front of the room stood the pulpit, and behind it was the smallest choir loft you could imagine—a few feet wide and a few feet deep. On each side of the loft were two six-by-six rooms. One room served as the pastor's study and the other room was where the choir would gather.

My most memorable times in that old church were thanks to my Sunday school teacher, Mrs. Georgie Tucker. She was a sweet and caring woman, who had such a wonderful way of making sure that we actually learned something during her brief time with us each week. We would pile in the little room, and Mrs. Tucker would pull out her small book of ABC's and diligently walk us through a lesson that connected a letter of the alphabet to a character or subject in the Bible. For instance: *"A is for Adam, the very first man. B is for the Bible, the best book in the land. C is for Cain, D is for Daniel, E is for Eve, F is for Father, G is for God, H is for Heaven*, and so on. I thank God for the hundreds of men and women I've met all over the world like Mrs. Georgie Tucker, who take their time to speak words of Biblical wisdom to children

Our pastor would preach once a month, but we had Sunday school every Sunday. Once a month after Sunday school, the church congregation moved into the sanctuary for the worship service. When we were kids, there seemed to be lots of people in our little church, but as I walk into that modest structure today—yes, it's still standing—I realize that a couple dozen adults and a group of kids could have packed the pews. Everything seems bigger when you're young.

During my childhood we had a handful of pastors at Friendship Baptist. The first pastor I remember was Reverend S.M. Simpson. We also had visiting ministers, such as Reverend William Applegate, who was in his nineties when I first heard him in the pulpit. The dedicated minister was so frail that the deacons had to assist him up to and down from the lectern. Even as a child I recognized his love for God and his love for the Word.

It was under the teaching of Reverend S.M. Simpson that I became a Christian. He was truly dedicated to our church, and I later learned that he would drive for many miles to come to minister. Reverend Simpson and his wife consistently showed us kindness, and we knew they valued us.

The pastor that followed Reverend Simpson was Reverend Tommy Lee Hudspeth. Reverend Hudspeth and his wife, Mrs. Margie, served at our church from my early childhood until I graduated high school. Reverend Hudspeth left an impression on me one night when my dad and I paid an unexpected visit to his home and we found him studying his Bible by the light of a kerosene lantern. Until that moment, as a child I had only seen preachers in church and behind the pulpit. To see him in the Word at his home demonstrated to me that my pastor was a true man of God. As I look back now, I realize his character was impacting my life, and he was a mentor even when he wasn't aware. He had never attended a Bible college to be a minister. He was a student of the

Word and grew up in an era when men simply felt the Lord's call and followed Him.

Our little church provided us kids with colorful entertainment that came from some of its members. There was an elderly lady who would open her umbrella inside the church when the sun would shine on her. Although that was strange behavior, she simply went about her business as if it were not. Because we didn't understand things like dementia or Alzheimer's, I made it a point not to sit too close to her.

My siblings and I sat on the other side of the church near an older gentleman, who after falling asleep, would begin to drool. Actually, we called it "slobbering." For some unknown reason my siblings and I found it more acceptable to sit by a man who drooled rather than a woman with an open umbrella in God's house.

Later, I realized the richness of the community I was a part of. Some of the teachers in our church were educators: Professor Bailey, Mr. John Q. Adams, and Elizabeth Smith, to name a few. Some were professors at a local black college called Morris Booker. They imparted biblical and academic knowledge to us.

When we weren't sitting in the congregation, my siblings and I sat in the tiny choir loft. I loved singing and always have. It was something that came very naturally to me, and I enjoyed belting out a good song in church.

We gathered in the pastor's room adjacent to the stage, and we would look to see which side of the church our mother and dad were sitting. We would know which side of the choir loft we should sit on in order to stay out of their view based upon the pew they had chosen. During a long-winded sermon in a hot country church it was not uncommon for one or more of the Graham children to fall asleep and we didn't want our parents to see us. On cue, we would scramble, push, and wrestle our way to the opposite wall out of our parents' sight. That back corner seat in the choir was the best place to lean my head against the wall and nod off.

I will never forget the simple things about attending church during my youth. I remember walking to church with my entire family on Sunday mornings. Sunday evenings when we went to B.T.U. (Baptist Training Union), the grasshoppers were jumping and the crickets filled the air with their sounds. The sincere preaching, the thoughtful teaching, and the colorful experiences I had in that little church blessed me beyond measure and have proved to be the strong foundational moments on which I built the rest of my life of faith.

I really appreciate how most churches have matured. These days, the term "white church" might sound a little strange to some people, and it saddens me to say that, unfortunately, the term is still alive today. But the terms "black church" and "white church" were always used in the South. When I was a young teen, I got invited to a white church in my community. I'm sure it came as no surprise to my brothers and sisters that I would be the one to break through the color barrier. I was up for always taking the "road less traveled."

I put on my fresh, clean shirt and tied a tie around my neck. I made sure my shoes were clean, and I put on a suit. As always, I wanted to look my best and honor God. I was going to a youth meeting at a white church, and my entrance and presence there would be memorable. With no fear, I walked into the youth room and looked for my friend Mark, who had invited me. Seeing the other students at the meeting wearing jeans, T-shirts, and sneakers, and there I was, dressed to the nines, I took off my jacket, took off my tie, and I sat with my good friend, Mark. I anticipated the stares, but what I didn't anticipate was being with students and enjoying God together.

CHAPTER 10

"School"

Before the schools were integrated in the South, I spent my elementary education years at an all-black rural school. I never really thought about whether or not my education was at the same level as the white school in town. I was just happy to be attending school. Being a poor kid in my school was not out of the ordinary. In fact, it was the norm. Much of my community lived at or below the poverty line. As a young boy, I would see evidence of being poor, but it only served to motivate me.

One of the highest priorities in my mom and dad's lives was a good education for their children. It was especially important to them. From the time we walked out the front door, to the time we returned home, Mother expected us to be learning. First, Mother made sure we were clean. That meant the boys wore pressed and creased blue jeans, and the girls wore clean, and ironed dresses, and white bobby socks. The girls also had ribbons and bows in their hair. After our shoes were tied and our hair was neatly combed, Mother would instruct us to sprinkle some baking soda on a wet towel and clean our teeth.

Mom must have started her days very early before sending us to school. She would cook a couple dozen eggs and two large pans of homemade biscuits for us to eat every morning. I remember Mother pulling the Pacific Jack mackerels out of the can. They were silver and blue and very shiny. She would then fashion the oily fish meat into a dollar pancake-sized patty.

As delicious as that may sound to some people, I could only consume the slimy fish if I poured T.J. Blackburn syrup all over them. Thinking back now to the mackerel patty covered in maple syrup, I wonder how I made it through school.

I took lunch in a brown paper bag. Inside the bag I would find the biscuits and the mackerel patties she had prepared that morning for our main course. I suppose these days they may be considered a fancy food.

We headed off to school each day as if school could not exist without a Graham in the classroom. It didn't matter how many ailments we had, it was a given that we would drag ourselves out of bed in order to attend school. That's how important Mother made perfect attendance in school seem to us. At the end of the school year, it was one of our greatest moments to receive the perfect attendance certificate. What joy and pride it brought to Mom and Dad when they saw each of their children holding his or her perfect attendance certificate.

They knew that the small commitment of attending each day would build character and confidence for life. They knew that going to school even when we didn't feel well taught us perseverance. They showed me how good it was to have someone believe in me.

Mom and Dad impressed upon us several life lessons as they congratulated us for being in class and learning each time the school doors were open. It was important to commit to a task and carry it out to the best of our abilities. Mom and Dad taught us to finish what we started and that principle has proven to be a valuable life lesson for me.

Before we moved within walking distance of the school, we had to ride a bus. Some of my fondest memories are of hurrying to catch the school bus at the end of Skipper Bridge. Because there were so few students on our route, the school assigned us the "short bus." The short bus was like an ordinary full-sized school bus, but it looked as if someone had taken a saw and cut it in half. Because the short bus had been traditionally used to transport the physically disabled, you can imagine how we all felt as we arrived at school and stepped off the bus to schoolyard teasing.

Another memory is of sitting in my first grade class, with my eyes locked on Velmatine, my first crush. To my young heart, she was the prettiest girl in my school. Something about those ribbons in her hair caught my eye, and I would look forward to lunch so I could talk to her. At lunch I would offer her my mackerel sandwich, which is probably one reason why no long-term relationship lasted beyond the first grade.

But it wasn't just Velmatine that kept my mind wandering while in school. I was a dreamer, like most little kids in school. My dreams always entailed a big, beautiful house to live in, lots of money to spend, and endless travel around the world. I believe Miss Gertrude Hawthorne, my second grade teacher, encouraged those thoughts and dreams. She was constantly sharing pictures of her summer travels to places like the Grand Canyon and the California redwoods. When she told me there was a tree big enough for a car to drive through, it amazed me. Her stories and pictures were fantastic in my mind and helped to fuel a sense of adventure in me.

Another way my teacher Mrs. Hawthorne impacted the direction of my life was her interest in public speaking. She had no idea at the time that her encouraging me to stand in front of the class and recite a poem was setting in motion the use of one of my gifts I have used in my profession for over forty years.

"Charles, I want to take you around to each of the classrooms and have you recite the poem you have learned," she informed me with a sense of pride.

Mrs. Hawthorne was very impressed with not only my ability to memorize and recite the poem, but my natural flare for dramatic interpretation. With her leading the way, I set out on my first performance tour. Down the halls and into the various classes I went, reciting the poem and bringing joy and a thrill to my teacher, who was showing me off to the rest of the school.

Each teacher gladly interrupted his or her class and introduced me. I stood proudly and began my recitation.

One day when I went visiting,
A little lamb was there.
I picked it up and held it tight.
It didn't seem to care.
Its wool was soft and felt so warm,
Like sunlight on the sand.
And when I gently put it down,
It licked me on the hand.

Those were the delightful verses I had memorized, and the children in each of the classrooms seemed to enjoy my performance. Meanwhile, Mrs. Hawthorne nodded and beamed as my tiny second-grader voice filled each room. She was the proud instructor, and I was her prize pupil. It was education at its finest for Mrs. Hawthorne. I loved the applause, and I really loved the smiles and feedback I was getting from the kids. I also enjoyed the thoughtful nods of encouragement from the teachers. By the time my school tour made it to the sixth graders, I was swelling with confidence and perhaps an overdose of pride.

The younger students were calm and more impressed by someone of my age performing without fear. *The big sixth graders, needed a performance*, I thought to myself. They were so much older than me, and I figured that they would not be so easily impressed by my cuteness. When I saw them staring at me with their upper-classmen judgment, I knew I had to put a humorous spin on my little kid poem.

The last line of the poem that I had been using for the first five elementary grades was,

> *When I gently put it down,*
> *It licked me on the hand.*

It was a peaceful picture of a docile lamb licking my hand. However, in my gut I knew that line wouldn't go over well with the big kids. In order to spare myself the embarrassment and the eye rolling from the more mature sixth graders, I suddenly changed the line:

> When I gently put it down,
> It bit off my left hand!

The sixth graders burst into laughter, and I beamed with delight. My spur-of-the-moment twist of the verse was a hit.

Unfortunately for me, my fifteen minutes of fame was short-lived. Mrs. Hawthorne was shocked, embarrassed, and humiliated that her prize student had thrown her an unexpected poetic curve ball. To my surprise, that event led to a paddling from the same woman who earlier in the day could only sing my praises. And with those swats my poetry career came to a screeching halt, but the good feeling of getting up in front of people and performing stuck in my mind. I liked it. It was a natural feeling for me, and I wanted more.

My fourth grade teacher, Miss Mary Lou Walker, was also a music and art teacher at my school. She had a profound impact on my life as a person and performer. There were many attributes she possessed that endeared her students to her, but the fact that she had developed talents in both music and painting captured my attention. She was a wonderful piano player, who seemed to bring grace and ease to her music. When I discovered that she could paint as well, I was even more impressed. But it wasn't just her expression on the keys or the graceful stroke of her paintbrush that drew me to her; it was also her upbeat and cheerful attitude about life. She brought her happiness and a positive attitude into the classroom, and that was refreshing in a school full of strict rules.

We learned seasonal songs at Thanksgiving, Christmas, and springtime. Miss Walker had a unique situation in the school because her classroom had a piano, which meant she could play it when she wished. When a tune entered her mind and it had some connection to the subject she was teaching, she would sit at the piano and let the keys do the teaching.

I will never forget when Miss Carrie Pugh became our new music teacher. She was the first person to introduce me to songs such as *Climb Every Mountain*, from the musical *The Sound of Music*. Songs from Broadway were so full of story and expression, and they provided an interesting departure from the church songs I was used to hearing. Although I enjoy songs with spiritual themes, I am thankful that Miss Pugh appreciated various kinds of music and widened my musical horizons. I am proud to say that the wonderful teacher who exposed me to beautiful, classic songs is still my friend to this day.

A great joy for me has been being able to share my life of music ministry and travels with several of the teachers who made such an impact on who I am. I didn't realize as a child just how much my teachers and their interests would so powerfully affect my life. Today, I'm so thankful that they shared what they loved with me.

When you grow up in a family with lots of siblings, you realize later in life that your childhood was never experienced alone. We woke up in the morning and got ready for school together. We boarded the short bus or walked together. We saw each other in the halls, at lunchtime, and during recess. I wouldn't trade the camaraderie created between my siblings and me for anything.

If there were one thing I could change about my elementary school days, it would be school picture day. Picture days always had some degree of excitement for some reason. I knew I wanted to look my best for an image that I would be stuck with forever.

Most students worried about their hair, their face, their teeth, and their jewelry. But, most of all, they worried about what article of clothing they would wear. We had to use our ingenuity when it came to the proper clothing for pictures. Shirts and tops were handed down to the next in line if they had any semblance of use left in them. But when it came to school picture day, nobody wanted to wear some questionable, worn-out old shirt or sweater that would be forever captured on film.

One year, Mother hatched an ingenious plan for a decent picture. My brother Stanley and I shared a green and tan wool sweater. Because it was the best garment we had, Mother sent us off with the plan that we would both have our pictures taken wearing the sweater. Stanley's class got their pictures taken first. The plan was simple: Stanley would wear the sweater for his picture sitting, and then after his picture was taken, he would hustle the sweater to me. It was as if we were competing in a relay race. He took off the sweater, and I threw it on as fast as I could in order to stand in line with my class.

When it came time for me to have my photo taken, I stepped in front of the camera as instructed. The photographer raised an eyebrow and gave me the strangest look. He shook his head and said, *Smile.* I couldn't figure out why the photographer had such a strange look on his face. *Was it the sweater? Did I have something stuck in my teeth?*

It wasn't until we got our pictures back that I saw why the photographer had such a look on his face. We ran from school back to our home where Mother was waiting anxiously to see our pictures. We gathered around Mom and we handed our pictures to her for her approval. Joyce handed hers to Mother first.

"Oh, Joyce. That's nice," she said as she admired Joyce's image and her pretty smile.

Next, Mother looked at Wanda's photo.

"Oh, Wanda. That's nice," Mother nodded her approval.

She took Stanley's picture from his hand.

"Oh, Stanley. That's nice," Mother said with another big smile and nod.

And then, I gave my picture to my mother. Like the photographer, she looked at my photo and raised an eyebrow in surprise.

After a moment she finally said, "Oh, Charles. That's you."

It was clear that the perfect picture scheme had a few flaws. The bow tie I had quickly clipped to my collar was at a tortured angle. And the two-toned green sweater I shared with Stanley needed some straightening as well. What I thought looked good ended up being a crooked smile and a sad face. Needless to say, I didn't give out any pictures that year.

When I entered junior high, it was 1970, the first year of school integration. I rode the bus that took me from the farm community into the town of Dermott. The bus picked up all the students in the rural community— both blacks and whites.

Because of integration, the former black school in Dermott had been re-purposed and reassigned to be the new junior high school for all students. For the first time in our little town's history, the former white high school had become the new high school for all races. It was an extreme change for me. At this time in my life, I didn't know any of the white students. I had hardly traveled into Dermott, which was only five miles away from my house.

The new Dermott junior high school was where I started the seventh grade. Our newly integrated school also had black and white teachers. It seems strange, but white and black teachers didn't work together in the same school before that year.

Suddenly, the school year offered me a flood of changes. It was one of those strange moments in life when I had nothing to measure it by. All I knew was I had transitioned from a little school full of black students whom I knew and who knew me, to a big school with black and white students and teachers. It was a first for me to change classrooms when the bell rang, and it was also a first for me to make new friends of another race.

I believe that one of the biggest things that helped me adjust was the fact that nearly everything was different, so I didn't just focus on the inter-racial aspect of the experience. For the most part, the junior high teachers were rolling with the changes, but there did seem to be a difference in their demeanor. Teachers were cordial. I can remember one teacher in particular who would allow himself to be nice, but not too personal. It seemed we had moved from tender and compassionate teachers to impersonal professionals who had made the choice to be instructors and not friends.

I suppose the strangest event that happened during the integration transition was when an ugly rumor began to work its way through the town. The word on the street was that a race riot was about to explode on campus. Before long, black and white parents arrived at the school to get their children and take them home. For me, the rumors didn't seem to make an impact. I stayed in my classroom with a white friend and we talked as the anxious activity took place all around us. Barbara and I enjoyed a nice long conversation and tried to forget the anxiousness of the day. I recently visited with Barbara's mother, and she thanked me for assuring her I would not let anything happen to her daughter. I was surprised that a simple act of kindness made such an impression on her.

I'm also glad that my parents taught me character as a young boy.

I consider myself fortunate today as I look back and realize I had a front row seat to the social changes that were happening in my hometown and in America. What I experienced firsthand helped me to develop a social consciousness. I gained awareness in my life that caused me to think beyond the small town in which I lived and beyond the limits of being raised poor. It caused me to dream beyond the cultural and economic limitations that were always before me. I began to dream of ways that would propel me out of my circumstances.

The social consciousness prompted me to ask questions of teachers, parents, and myself. I wasn't trying to be a troublemaker or stir up controversy; I just thought that I deserved some straight answers regarding why things were done the way they were done. To give myself a little more credibility, I decided to run for class officer. That would give me a solid voice in my high school's student government. One of the first issues I brought up to the school principal was why it was necessary to have both a white captain and a black captain of the football team. I found out pretty quickly why. When the homecoming game approached and the queen candidates were chosen, the administration wanted to make sure that whoever kissed the homecoming queen was of the same race. The answer that I received regarding most uncomfortable questions such as that was, *That's the way we have to do it*. In retrospect, I realize that was the nature of the environment in which we lived. That phrase was the code words for saying they couldn't approve of a mixed-race kiss.

One day, I boldly asked my typing teacher a pointed question. Again, it wasn't because I was wrestling with a black and white issue. It was a spiritual issue for me.

"If I came to your church this Sunday, what would happen?" I asked.

She thought for a moment and then sadly replied, "If you came to my church, people would walk out."

Although I wasn't surprised at her reply, I was saddened by that thought. I imagined walking into her church and watching men and women grabbing their children's hands and ushering them out the door, all because of the color of my skin. It's a sobering thought.

As I looked at my teacher, she bowed her head and began to cry. My question had struck a nerve, and it forced us to admit that the church culture in which we choose to worship was not designed to lift up the love of Jesus Christ, but rather it demonstrated tangibly that we excluded people Jesus would have embraced. I have to admit it was not just the culture of some white churches, but could also be seen in some black churches.

After confronting my typing teacher, I approached my shop teacher, who was a Christian and who always witnessed to his class. I asked him the same question.

"What would happen if I came to your church?"

He thought for a moment and replied, "If I was the deacon greeting you at the front door that Sunday, I'd have to refuse your entrance."

His answer still troubles me today. He shook his head and said, "Charles, that's why we have white churches and black churches. That's just the way it is."

There were also black teachers who held the same view of not accepting whites at their church. My attitude at that time was simple. If a person was not a Christian, I could understand their prejudice. However, if a person claimed to be a Christian, I wondered how in the world they could carry such an attitude toward another human.

Black history class was offered at our newly integrated high school and was taught by Mr. Charles Scurlock. He was given the task of teaching students the history of blacks in America. I appreciated his approach as he shared important information that both blacks and whites needed to know. Although it could have gotten uncomfortable with white students and black students sitting inches from each other, he never dismissed his responsibilities of presenting the truth. He focused on teaching about blacks in America's history and celebrating their contributions, without fueling hostility or resentment in the classroom.

He didn't use phrases such as, *All whites were like this*, or *All blacks were like that*. Because he lived without prejudice, he taught us truth from his personal convictions. His character helped me learn how to approach the differences without prejudice.

The Future Farmers of America classroom was detached from the main school building, and the porch of the FFA building was like the barbershop. It was a place for the guys to gather and brag about their weekend of drinking and girls. Their stories never matched my quiet and uneventful weekends.

Yeah, ummm ... I stayed home and ... baby-sat my little brothers and sisters. I fed the hogs and watched some TV. That was my typical response.

I began dreading going to school on Monday morning because there was no way to get past the bragging guys. I tried hard to avoid them and even timed my arrival so I would show up to class the minute it began.

One weekend, I had an encounter with the Lord, and He encouraged me to go to school and declare my faith to those guys. The enemy was saying, *Don't do that. You will be laughed at. They will ridicule you.* But I knew I had to act on what God was telling me to do. I had to be bold. I had to speak up and let the guys know what I believed and the life I had chosen to live.

The following Monday, I arrived early for class and waited for the other guys to gather. When they got there, they began laughing and talking about drinking and exploits with girls as usual.

When they asked what I did over the weekend, I replied honestly and said, "I went to church this weekend."

"Oh, man! Church? Come on, man," the guys laughed and taunted me.

"Yes. I go to church every weekend. And, I served as a delegate for our Sunday school convention."

You should have seen the looks on their faces. I was all in. All my cards were on the table. God wanted me to be bold and confident, and that's what I was.

"Charles Graham, you're crazy."

The guys broke into laughter and made fun of my attending church. My greatest fears were realized. However, something very different happened after class. The bell rang, and everyone started filing out of the classroom. That's when a classmate named, Maurice, walked up to me and unexpectedly said,

"I knew you were a Christian, Charles."

"You did?" I asked.

"Yes. I just wondered when you would tell the truth."

Maurice and I walked on to our next class, and I felt good because I had stayed true to who I was in the Lord. That moment solidified our friendship.

One day, Maurice and I decided to play a prank on a substitute teacher. Our teacher Mrs. Buckner was absent. Maurice and I got the bright idea that we would trade seats and identities. Maurice would be Charles, and I would be Maurice. It was the perfect plan to pull one over on the unsuspecting "sub." At the end of the class, we were proud of ourselves, thinking we had pulled off the prank without a hitch. To our surprise, the substitute teacher approached us unexpectedly before we exited the classroom.

The teacher looked at me and remarked, "I really enjoyed the speech you gave in church yesterday."

I gulped as the guilt rushed through my body. Our substitute teacher had been in the church service and she heard me speak. She knew I was "Charles Graham," and not Maurice.

"You lied in class today, and I'm disappointed."

Teachers and parents have a way of penetrating your heart when they use phrases such as, *You disappointed me*, or *I believe in you*. That day, I learned to be mindful of my actions. People are watching, and even if it isn't fair at times, they are judging whom you claim to be.

I wasn't athletic, so I did everything I could to avoid physical education (PE) class, even to the point of delaying the class until my senior year. PE was a required credit for graduation. Despite my protesting that I was battling a self-diagnosed "floating kidney" and I should not participate in any strenuous physical activity, my pleas fell on deaf ears. I even appealed to a doctor to see if he could write me a note confirming my alleged floating kidney. Even the doctor would not save me from a PE class.

I suppose I ended up making the best of a bad situation. Because I took PE my senior year, I was the oldest in the class full of freshmen. The teacher put me in charge of running the games and activities. So, in a way, I did avoid having to participate. One day I took my newfound confidence a step too far. Some of my friends were involved with intramural basketball, and I got the crazy notion that I should participate. I suppose I just wanted to fit in and have some fun.

Because I knew my siblings would ridicule me, I snuck out of the house with my sneakers, and I dressed for PE in the locker room. I walked out on the gym floor as if the star basketball player had just arrived, but in reality I was the most uncoordinated basketball player the student body had ever seen. I was the tallest guy on our team, so I jumped for the ball during the tip-off. I successfully tipped the ball, but unfortunately, I didn't know which goal was mine. I purposely stayed away from the action around the ball and remained near half court. Suddenly, the ball was thrown to me, and I had a clear path from half court to my goal. All I had to do was dribble the ball to the goal and make a layup.

But that was a problem because I didn't know how to dribble a ball. So I turned toward the empty goal and launched the ball. Let's just say that I would have had a better chance of scoring had I attempted to dribble. The ball sailed by, nowhere near the goal, and it bounced miserably off the court and into the stands.

That memorable, wild shot was the end of my intramural career. I can still hear the loud laughter from everyone in the gymnasium.

My love for art and music continued to flourish. Drawing and painting put me in a comfort zone as a teenager. I spent a lot of time in the school gym creating and painting banners for sports events. For me, it was more than getting out of a class. Designing and painting a paper banner that the Dermott Rams players would burst through was just as much fun as participating in the game. When the banner was unfurled, I loved that my community at the football and basketball games got to see my contribution to collective school pride.

When I was in the tenth grade, I got a job as a janitor for the school. It gave me more responsibility, and for the first time I was making money doing something other than farm work. The solitude of working alone was enjoyable to me. The head of maintenance gave me a key to the storage room and to the school as well. Along with my responsibilities to make each room presentable for the teachers next morning, I was responsible for locking up the school when I was finished cleaning. Mother had trained me well to work hard, and it paid off when I was given the job.

One day, a fellow student named David approached me and asked if I would like to have a job at a local clothing store. Abrams was one of the two department stores in Dermott, and I was thrilled to be asked. I later learned the owner of Abrams had asked specifically for a black young man who could relate to Abrams's black clientele.

When I started the job, I discovered I would be performing the same tasks I was doing at the school. I was the guy in charge of keeping the store clean. Mom and Dad had trained me correctly to be polite and to work hard. Those two qualities, plus several others, prepared me to interact with the public, and Barry, the owner, was quick to see those attributes. When things got busy in the store, I interacted with customers and made some sales. Within two weeks of having the job, I was allowed to work as a salesperson, as well as clean the store.

The job in the store helped me to find some purpose in my life. Working with and around people was comfortable and felt more like destiny for me. I was at ease speaking in front of others, regardless the size of the gathering. That talent led to my becoming the Vice President of Future Farmers of America. I joined because one of my instructors, Mr. Floyd Gray, was full of personality and very engaging. He was outgoing and took a genuine interest in his students.

The athletes had their influential role models. Coaches were powerful and served as surrogate fathers to many of the athletes. Mr. Gray saw in me someone who could have another kind of pursuit besides sports. He saw my leadership qualities, and immediately I was encouraged to become an officer in the chapter.

Each FFA chapter took part in the national contest. I was encouraged to participate in the public speaking portion of the competition. The contests between chapters included things such as welding, forestry, animal husbandry, and in my case, public speaking. Mr. Gray put me through lots of speaking drills to help me improve and gain confidence.

After winning the public speaking contest at a local level, I advanced to the state level of the competition, held in Arkansas's capitol, Little Rock.

During 1973-74, my junior year, we left our little town, and we went to the big city—Little Rock, Arkansas. It was there that I got to stay in a hotel for the first time. It was also in the hotel I experienced for the first time what riding in an elevator felt like. It's interesting in the hustle and bustle of the modern life in which I live and operate today, how easy it is to forget what impressions such firsts make upon a person. There are people, both young and old, in Dermott today who have a host of firsts that they need to experience in order to see how much life has to offer.

Just as I have several music teachers in my past to thank for encouraging me to sing, I also have Mr. Gray to thank for encouraging me to stand before an audience and speak with articulation and logic.

It was during my junior year that tragedy struck our family; a stroke disabled Dad. His years of hard work came to a sudden and bitter end. It wasn't long before the landowner felt forced to let my dad go, which also meant we would have to move off the land and find another place to live.

Although I was seventeen, I'm not sure I grasped all the ramifications his sudden physical disability would mean to us. The once strong and energetic man was paralyzed down one side of his body. As I looked at my father, a mix of emotions moved through me.

During this difficult time Mother was working in the school cafeteria. A sweet Christian white lady who worked alongside my mom shared our plight with her husband. The Connards owned a house in town and felt that God had impressed upon them to sell it to my mom and dad. The generous offer was for my parents to pay them fifty dollars a month and for us to move in immediately. The house would be very convenient for my mother, who would be maintaining a job as a school cook, as well as cooking for a local white family. When Mom and Dad agreed to purchase the house, it was the first time in their lives they would own a home.

Another glimpse of the world beyond Dermott came later during my junior year. A fellow classmate, Tyana, and I were invited to a college weekend at Oral Roberts University in Tulsa, Oklahoma. I had been given a book to read called *The Miracles of Seed Faith*, written by Dr. Oral Roberts, president and founder of Oral Roberts University. When I was given that powerful book, the seed planted in me was the dream of attending a Christian university. So when I was presented with the opportunity to visit the university, it was a dream come true.

I had a literature teacher, Miss Julia Carter, who was considered to be dramatic and a bit eccentric by some. I loved her personality and we connected as friends. When I told her that I was going to take a Greyhound bus ride to Tulsa to visit ORU, she was thrilled. She insisted on taking me to Wiseman's department store to buy me a new lavender paisley tie for the occasion. You can imagine my eyes when I looked at the price tag that read $40.00.

I felt as if I were in a scene from *The Wizard of Oz* as we approached the ORU campus in Tulsa.

"I'm not in Arkansas anymore," I said to myself.

I was impressed by the modern architecture and the beautiful landscape at the prestigious Christian university. When I saw ORU's huge towers, the gold glass buildings, and the campus brimming with happy students, I was filled with excitement.

On campus the hosts showed me the dorms and the various buildings that could be my home for four years once I graduated high school in Dermott. I imagined myself walking the sidewalks as an ORU student with books under my arm, heading to classes. *I wondered if this could be it.*

During the campus visit, the World Action Singers treated us to a free concert. I saw a diverse group of students in the choir, which gave me even more confidence that God had put me in a place where I could fit in and discover more of my potential.

It would be an understatement to say that I had a good time on the trip. My friend and I were on cloud nine as the visit ended and we took the long bus ride home to southeast Arkansas. All I could do was thank God as I kept projecting my thoughts to the next year, when I would get my high school diploma, pack my bags, and head to ORU. I couldn't wait to submit my application to Oral Roberts. I would be the first in the family to attend college and pursue a degree.

The summer before my senior year, my relationship with several of the white students in school continued to grow. Because of those friendships I was invited to a party held at the local racquet club in town that had tennis courts and a swimming pool. It was a private club built to counter the mixing of the races in the public swimming pool.

One of the friends I met while at that party was a guy named Robert. Everyone who knew him called him "Bubba." His parents had been missionaries in Africa, and his dad was back in the United States serving as an associational missionary.

Bubba was polite, and there was something different about him. We hung out together all summer, and a very strong friendship began. Bubba and I had art class and choir together. He told me all about his friends and life in Africa as I shared with him about my simple life on a cotton farm.

My senior year was the fall of 1974 and the spring of 1975. In order to make the most of it, I decided to run for president of the senior class. During each of my years in high school, I had run for either president or vice president and won. I had some stiff competition my senior year for class president as a smarter and much more popular guy decided to enter the election. The vote was close, and the administration held a runoff to see who could emerge as a clear winner. Rufus, my opponent, was smart and well liked by the teachers. I really wanted the honor of being president my senior year, so I went all out using my artistic skills to create eye-catching Charles Graham posters that could dominate the halls and classrooms. Somehow, I managed to beat Rufus, and when I gave my acceptance speech to the student body, I was in my element. I loved getting up in front of everyone and telling my classmates all about my vision for the school.

Life was moving along nicely during my senior year when one day a business-sized envelope arrived in the mail. On the upper-left corner of the envelope was the unmistakable return address from Oral Roberts University. This was it: the moment I had been waiting for. It was the key to unlock my future as a student at ORU. I recalled the gleaming campus with its unique, modern architecture. I saw myself walking on the sidewalks with other new students, preparing for a Christian life, and serving the Lord.

You are accepted academically, but ...

I stared at the formal white stationery that informed me that I had been accepted; however, due to my family's financial status, attending Oral Roberts would not be in my future. After I read the letter, I shared the disappointing news with Bubba. He read the letter and he could see how devastated I was.

"Charles, don't worry about it. God's in control."

The next day, Bubba approached me and told me that his mom and dad would like to invite me to dinner. It was my first invitation to dine in a white person's home. It was my pleasure to go to Bubba's house, where it was just his family and I sitting at the dinner table.

"Bubba says you got some disappointing news today?" Reverend Garvin asked.

"Yes, sir, I did."

"And your heart is still set on attending college?"

"It is. I want to study art."

"I represent a college, and I keep my eyes out for good students like you. I'm a courier for Southwest Baptist College in Bolivar, Missouri. You may have never heard of it, but it's an excellent college. I'd be happy to submit your name and get the ball rolling."

"That's where I'm going," Bubba chimed in.

"Oh. Well, yes, that would be great. Thank you, Reverend Garvin," I answered with some excitement.

"My pleasure. Keep up your good attitude and your good grades."

Honestly, I was caught off guard. I wasn't used to someone offering me something. I had no idea what a courier was, but it sounded pretty important. The words and the tone of Reverend Garvin's voice reassured me that perhaps my dream of attending a Christian college wasn't over. I never imagined the impact a new student named "Bubba" could have on my life.

It wasn't long after that dinner with Bubba's family that my brother Curtis and my mother drove me from Dermott to a little town in Southwest Missouri called Bolivar. I was scheduled to attend a campus tour of Southwest Baptist College; a four-year liberal arts Christian school nestled in the Missouri Ozarks. My arrival to the school was a culture shock. Dermott and the surrounding areas were approximately 60% black and 40% white. When we drove through Springfield, Missouri, on our way to Bolivar, folks in the cars were 100% white.

My brother accelerated the car, and as we passed the garbage truck, he remarked jokingly,

"I'm going to pass this garbage truck, Charles. I'll feel better if there's a black guy driving it."

Mom and I did the old corner-of-the-eye glance to see if the garbage truck driver was black.

"He's white!" Curtis said as he shook his head and we laughed. "Charles, if you come up missing, I'm not coming to look for you," he added.

I noticed the look of concern on my mom's face.

"I'll be fine, Mom. Students from all over the world come to Southwest Baptist College."

Our visit to the school couldn't have gone better. Mom, Curtis, and I toured the campus, and the more I saw, the more I felt in my heart it was where God wanted me to be. We walked through the halls of the music and art building, and the feelings grew stronger. Muffled sounds of musical instruments and singing voices could be heard coming from rehearsal rooms. Each rehearsal room door had a narrow vertical window, and I had to peer into each one to see and listen to students rehearsing. By the time I reached my advisor's office, I was ready to sign any document the school wanted signed. I loved the atmosphere.

My counselor at Southwest Baptist was an art instructor named Dr. Larry Root. He was a warm and friendly professor who connected with me immediately. There was a true sense of professionalism in his manner, and I could tell that he was an example of what a Christian university professor should be. He seemed genuinely concerned and interested in what I wished to make of myself.

Next, we toured the dorms and the student union, as well as many of the buildings where I would be continuing my education. All I could think of was how I would be the first in the family to ever attend college. I wished that I could simply stay at Southwest Baptist and send for my things, but I had to return home and finish high school. My first day of college would arrive soon enough.

CHAPTER 11

"My Community and Me"

Family, church, school, and community were the four things that laid the foundation for who I was and who I have become. In all four of these categories, I learned slowly but surely who I was and how I either fit in or didn't fit in as I grew up in Dermott. My junior and senior years in high school became the years when the height of my spiritual awareness and the sense of community converged.

I will never forget the day I was walking to my job at Abrams clothing store and a car stopped alongside of me. The woman in the car got my attention.

"Excuse me," the lady called out to me as she continued rolling down her window.

"Yes, ma'am?"

"Young man, come here for a moment, please."

Although this was an unusual thing to happen to me, I left the sidewalk and walked to her car.

"Yes, ma'am?"

"The Lord just showed me something about you," she said in her quiet voice.

I'm sure I must have had a curious look on my face. It was not a common occurrence having people stop me on the street to tell me that God had communicated something to them about me. The next words out of her mouth were not only surprising to me then, but what she said still amazes me as I think back on it today.

"Young man, God showed me that one day you're going to be standing in front of thousands of people. God is going to use you to minister to people. And, I will be praying for you," she told me.

I thanked her, and she nodded and drove away, leaving me with a bewildered look on my face. As I watched her car disappear around the corner, her words sank deep within my spirit. *Standing in front of thousands of people?* How strange it was to get a word like that from a complete stranger. With 20/20 hindsight, I can look back from where I am now and say with confidence that the word she had gotten from the Lord was absolutely correct. At that time, neither of us had any idea what it meant, but the path that God had for me to walk included my becoming a singing minister, and the "thousands of people" to which she referred would be men, women, boys, and girls from several different countries on three different continents!

That sweet lady could have kept the information to herself. She could have left her window up and not spoken to a young boy walking down the sidewalk. I have since learned that our lives are made up of moments whereby we step outside of our comfort zone and connect with someone else. At God's direction, we stop at curious moments to act within His perfect will.

Another experience standing in front of large crowd and speaking was when I entered an oratorical contest sponsored by our local Optimist Club in Dermott. Because I had earned a spot in the state competition, I was invited to give my speech at the local Optimist Club dinner. You can imagine the thrill for my parents and me as we prepared to attend the dinner held in the Circle K restaurant. I'll never forget the look on my dad's face when he bought himself a new sport coat for my special evening.

For the first time in my life, we would be allowed to walk through the front door of the restaurant and sit in the dining area to have our meal. It was common to see black people at the back door ordering and receiving their food.

Mom and Dad were bursting with pride as I stood up and delivered my speech in front of the audience made up of Dermott's business class. Mom looked beautiful in her Sunday best. Dad looked sharp in his new jacket, his eyes beaming with pride. I may not have excelled in sports as my father would have wished, but that night I know I brought immense pride into his life for lots of reasons, not just for winning the public speaking award.

Situations such as back doors, segregated schools, and separated doctors' offices were the nature of my community when I was a child and young man. I understood that reality. In spite of the community's condition, I came to the strong realization that no matter how bad it was or how bad it could get, God had a purpose for my life.

As each year passed, I realized that leaving my community was what God would want from me. Despite sleeping four to a bed, cutting wood in the winter, keeping the stove blazing, fetching water from a pump, using outdoor toilets, chopping, picking, and dragging cotton sacks, pushing to start Dad's car, sharing a secondhand bike, and wearing Stanley's sweater, the older I became, the more aware I was of God's love and plans. I would not be held captive to my circumstances or let them define who I wanted to be.

Even my job at Abrams shaped the way I viewed others. I observed how persons of all backgrounds thought of each other and how they treated one another.

At first the owner of the department store just wanted someone to clean the store, but within two weeks I was promoted to a salesperson. The owner of Abrams, Mr. and Mrs. Brunner, were Jewish. They offered me an opportunity to walk beyond the historical norms in the community. At the time, I considered Mr. Brunner to be just another white person in our community. I didn't understand the Jewish culture or how they had to deal with bias in our town. The more I worked at Abrams for the Brunners, the more I learned the importance of considering another person's worth.

As a young child, I walked through my experiences with naivety. Frankly, you don't know what you don't know. But as I grew intellectually through my adolescence, I started to understand that my family was poor, which meant I was poor. Being poor brought with it many challenges.

If I didn't feel well, my parents had home remedies to try to cure me. But if I got really sick, Mom and Dad took me to the doctor's office in town, and when we approached his office, there were two front doors. There were no signs posted. It was understood that we were to enter the door on the right—for blacks only.

Community forms us like clay. When I travel these days, I see that firsthand. Country folk may have a much different way about them than persons from Chicago, New York, Atlanta, or London. Southerners in the U.S. can be different from people in the Northern United States. It's not just the clothes we wear or the way we speak, but it is a lifestyle. A person also takes on the pace and rhythm of the town in which they live.

In Dermott, there were many wonderful black and white people living alongside my family and me—people with compassionate hearts. But because of the time period in our nation's history, people were not free to express how they really felt. They weren't comfortable living the truth inside them.

CHAPTER 12

"Off to College"

Before I launch into the heart of my college days, I feel that it is important for the reader to understand what happened to me in the summer of 1975. It will provide a better idea of how God directed me away from the cotton fields of south Arkansas. Like most students in my town, when the school year came to a close, it was time to find a job and make money for the year ahead.

For me, it meant working a restaurant job in St. Louis, Missouri. It may seem like an odd place for my summer employment, but my Uncle Julius, Dad's brother, lived in St. Louis and worked at the Lambert Airport. Uncle Julius had been a chef at the airport for over forty years, and everyone knew him.

To describe my uncle, I have to start with the fact that he was always the best dressed man in the room. You might say he was a sharply dressed gentleman. Most days he wore a suit and a tie and was rarely without his hat. Another distinction regarding my Uncle Julius was that he was quite a bit different from my family when it came to expressing his faith. He was what we called "sanctified."

"You're going to get sanctified if you go to work with Uncle Julius," my brothers and sisters teased.

"I am not!"

"Yes, you are! If you spend the summer up there in St. Louis and you go to Uncle Julius's church, you're

going to come back sanctified. You watch!" my sister
warned.

"You'll see," I replied defiantly.

For the readers who are unfamiliar with the
expression "sanctified," it was the term used in the South
similar to Pentecostals that were filled with the Holy
Spirit. They were quite a bit livelier than the people in my
Baptist church. I was looking at the job opportunity as a
chance to get out of Dermott and to make some money
for my freshman year in college. I wasn't worried about
becoming sanctified.

Uncle Julius used to visit my family on occasion,
and when he showed up, he was the talk of the farm. He
would arrive in a nice car, and he was always dressed
how we imagined a Hollywood movie star might dress.
As soon as he heard that I had graduated from high
school, he was on the telephone encouraging me to come
to work with him. Before long I was on a Greyhound bus,
and I was traveling north to the big city of St. Louis,
where I had a job and a room waiting for me at Uncle
Julius's house.

When I arrived in the city, it was a shock. There
seemed to be more people in my uncle's neighborhood
than in my entire town. I got settled into his home, and
the accommodations there were much better than at
home, where I had been sharing beds and bedrooms with
my siblings for years. And unlike my family's home in
Arkansas, it was quiet.

I had already made up my mind that on Sunday
morning there was no way I was going to attend my
uncle's church full of sanctified city folks. I had noticed a
Baptist church just around the corner from my uncle's
house, so that was where I decided to go. It was fine. It

was much bigger than what I was used to, and the service was uneventful. But when the next Sunday morning rolled around, I felt a pressing obligation to get up, get dressed, and attend my uncle's church. After all, he was being extremely nice to me. He had helped me with a job and provided me a place to live. When I informed him that I would be attending his church with him that morning and he was happy. I wasn't exactly sure what would take place in the Lively Stone Apostolic Church on St. Louis Avenue, but I knew that going to church with Uncle Julius was the right thing to do.

When we arrived, I went to a Sunday school class taught by Sister Roanne. She was a sweet and dedicated woman committed to teaching us the life lessons of Christ. After Sunday school the congregation gathered in the sanctuary for the main church service. My first impression was that everyone was nice, happy, and involved in the singing. The music was dynamic and full of a worshipful spirit. Bishop Scott's son played the organ, and a terrific pianist accompanied him. Also, a fantastic choir of men and women singing in four-part harmony was amazing to hear. Perhaps the biggest surprise for me was when communion was given. They served us real wine. At the end of the service, a nice police officer named Fred even walked up to me and introduced himself.

The best part of my morning was the welcoming attitude of all the youth in attendance. They were not shy at all about introducing themselves and making me feel as though I already belonged in their group. One of the many highlights of my time at that church was being a part of the youth group.

One day we gathered at the church and went as a group to Forest Park—a thirteen hundred acre park in the middle of St. Louis that is a little larger than Central Park in New York City. When we arrived, all of the youth got into a circle and prayed for God to bless our time together. The youth leader prayed that beyond our having a good time that we would be a witness for Jesus to people in the park. For the first time in my Christian experience, I saw young teens committed to being a reflection of who Jesus is. It hit me that the students were the ones leading the way, and not the older adults, who seemed to traditionally be the doers in churches I had been a part of. It was obvious that being a believer in the Lively Stone youth group was about much more than attending a church service. It was about living each day as an example of how Christ can change a person.

One night I sat alone in a pew and listened to the youth choir rehearsing. I took a moment, and I bowed my head in prayer. When I opened my eyes, the entire choir was standing around me. I learned that it was their intention that night to make sure I was filled with the Spirit. As I prayed, they gave me instructions. They wanted me to keep praying until I uttered a sound.

Finally, I uttered a sound.

"You've got it!" one of the choir members shouted.

And with that, the choir celebrated my being filled with the Spirit. I wasn't exactly sure what had happened, but I enjoyed it. After hugs and thank yous, I said goodbye to the choir, and I left the rehearsal.

When I arrived back in Dermott for a visit before moving away to college, my sister Wanda confronted me.

"There's something different about you, Charles," Wanda said with a nod.

"I met some young people at Uncle Julius's church who really love the Lord, and they're not afraid to show it. My spiritual life has been changed," I explained.

The morning of my departure to college arrived, and as I hugged everyone and said my goodbyes to my family, I felt as though my true journey of leaving Dermott and Arkansas had begun in earnest. One by one I hugged my family as if I were leaving on a trip across the world. In a sense, it was my true launch into the unknown, and things would never be the same for me.

"I'll be fine, Mother," I assured her as we hugged.

"I know," she smiled.

At that time, none of us said those three uncomfortable words, "I love you." The words were more comfortable to us when we communicated them in letters, or while speaking to one another on the telephone. It was an understanding that we had between us that we did indeed love one another. Later in life we would find those words easier to utter. The bond between us was strong and could not be broken. I looked into the loving eyes of each of my siblings with whom I had shared my childhood. We had so much in common. My older siblings and I had all dragged cotton bags behind us as we worked the fields on the farm. We had stood in the tiny choir loft on Sundays and had sung together. We had all felt the hugs from Mom, and we had all felt the belts on our backsides. Because of our common upbringing, we had the strongest of bonds between us. How blessed I felt to know that no matter what happened next, my life to that point was filled with acceptance and unconditional love from my family.

I looked into the eyes of my dad. For a couple of years, the stroke he suffered had reduced him from the hardest-working man I had ever known to a man who spent much of his time in a chair. Dad was the only one who did not show his emotion as I left, but I knew he loved me and would miss me.

After my brief visit with my family, I went back to St. Louis, and then a few days later I headed to Southwest Baptist College in Bolivar, Missouri. One of the men in the Lively Stone church kindly drove me to the small town in southwest Missouri. When I arrived at SWBC (later known as SBU), I had no idea of the protocol on campus for new students. I had no clue where I was to sign in, where I was supposed to be, or with whom I was supposed to speak. All I knew was that I was supposed to live on campus in a place called New Men's Dorm. I later found out why they called the dormitory "New Men's." It was the newest housing on campus for men, and they hadn't yet found a donor to name it after.

"Oh. You're Charles," the dorm mother remarked with some surprise in her voice.

"Yes, ma'am. Charles Graham."

"I'm Mom Riley."

She looked at me and then closely examined the paper she was holding. I could tell that something wasn't quite right by the way she looked at me.

"Hmmmm," she mumbled. "Okay, we'll get this figured out. Follow me."

I knew something was amiss, but she didn't explain herself. Mom Riley led me down a hallway, and I assumed we were headed to my new dorm room. We arrived at the room of the resident assistant, Jerry Steffy, a friendly upperclassman and preacher's kid who played on the baseball team.

"Jerry?" Mom called as she knocked on Jerry's door. "It's Mom Riley."

"Just a minute," Jerry called out from the other side of the closed door.

As Jerry prepared himself to open the door, Mom Riley and I stood silently in the hallway. It was awkward. Seconds seemed like several minutes until the door finally squeaked open.

"Jerry," Mom began, "this is Charles Graham. He's a new student from Arkansas—a freshman."

Jerry and I exchanged hellos, and Mom Riley continued, "We haven't made arrangements for his room just yet, and he needs a place to sleep for tonight."

Without hesitation, Jerry invited me in and showed me where I would be sleeping that night.

"It's just for tonight. I'll get it figured out in the morning," Mom assured us as she slowly closed the door.

Once Mom Riley left us, I began settling in. Jerry did not seem to have a problem with my being there. We hit it off immediately as he asked me lots of questions about what it was like where I'd come from. He asked about my family, as well as why I had chosen to come so far from home to attend college.

After lots of conversation, we agreed that it was time to turn in for the night. I got dressed for bed, and as I had been trained to do all my life, I knelt by the bed and began saying a prayer of thanksgiving. I wanted to thank God for the way He worked everything out to pave my way to get into college. I thanked Him again for my family. They were so proud of their first family member to leave the safety of the cotton fields and to venture off to attend college. It was a monumental time in all our lives. I found out later that my simple act of kneeling and praying by my bed made a huge impact on Jerry that night.

The next day, I awakened in a strange state, a strange town, a strange campus, and a stranger's dorm room. As my eyes blinked open, my prayer of thanksgiving picked up where it had left off. I had made it. The feeling in my heart at that awakening moment is hard to explain.

As promised, Mom Riley greeted Jerry and me with information regarding the room to which I would be assigned.

"The basketball players are all down on that wing of the dorm, Charles. That's where you'll be living," Mom Riley nodded.

It was blatantly obvious that the reason I would find my new accommodations on the basketball wing was because of the color of my skin. I had been introduced to Southwest Baptist through the missionary in my hometown and because of that, my ethnicity was not known. Again, I got that feeling in my chest that I had sensed many times before while growing up in Arkansas. I was immediately labeled because of my skin color, and not my character. However, before I reacted to Mom Riley's pronouncement, Jerry interrupted her.

"No, ma'am. Charles can stay here with me."

"With you? Jerry, you're the resident assistant. You get a room to yourself. You don't have to have a roommate."

"I know. But I have one now."

That first act of kindness and acceptance far away from home will never be forgotten. Jerry was from

Chicago, and interacting with African-American students wasn't foreign to him at all. In retrospect, he could have gone with the flow of protocol. He could have kept quiet and allowed me to move my things down to the basketball players' wing of the dormitory. He could have enjoyed the peace and quiet of a room to himself that semester.

I'm sure I would have managed and fit in just fine down the hall had Jerry not intervened. In fact, it wasn't long before I had befriended nearly all of the Bearcat basketball team. But God had other plans for how my university experience would begin, and Jerry's simple act of kindness was a big part of that beginning.

As I recall, my introduction into my new college environment and experience could be summed up in one word: "unprepared." I was not prepared for college in the fall of 1975, and frankly, Southwest Baptist College was not prepared for me. Unfortunately, I encountered things at SWBC that triggered negative thoughts and feelings inside me that I had hoped I left far behind in the Deep South. For example, when I entered Polk County, Missouri, that autumn day, the handful of black students attending Southwest Baptist accounted for most of the population of blacks in the entire county. I had been transplanted from a world of mixed race to a world where I stood out wherever I went, whether in church, at the supermarket, or just walking to class. The words of my brother Curtis haunted me: *If you get in trouble, don't expect me to come looking for you.*

Despite the negatives, I was on cloud nine. I was at the peak of my emotions because a life-long dream had come true and I was walking the sidewalks and halls of a college. The path had been prepared for me, and I was so proud and happy to be walking it. *Thank You, Lord,* was all I could hear in my mind.

As I walked through the music building, I heard young voices singing and musical instruments playing. As I continued past the classrooms, I could almost smell the creativity. God had placed me where I would begin my professional pursuit.

During those first days of college, I enjoyed strolling across the landscaped campus and seeing the smiling faces of other students from around the world. Saying "hello" and receiving a "hello" in return was easy and gratifying. I understood that I was not the only person walking the campus and carrying a big dream inside. It seemed as though everyone I met along my way was happy to be in school pursuing their personal goals.

Making friends was easy and instant for me. For instance, one of the guys in my dorm was an outgoing student from St. Louis named Steve. He was a tall guy who wore a leather jacket had long black hair. Steve and I conducted revivals together and he was there to support me when I received the news that my nephew had passed away. He drove me to Arkansas so I could be with my family through the tragedy. At SBU, guys, girls, faculty, and staff, seemed to be operating in a spirit of gladness, just like Steve. The friendly spirit on campus was contagious, and I was right where I wanted to be.

Perhaps the biggest event during my orientation week was participating in the talent show. The performance was open to anyone who wanted to put their talents on display for the entire student body. As a freshman, I did not know any better and didn't fully consider that many of the terrific upperclassmen were polished and trained singer-performers. I knew that I was being presented with a moment where I would stand on stage and sing. I signed up for the talent show, and my accompanist that night was a girl named Barbara.

"What would you like to sing?" she asked.

I froze. I thought for a few moments, and then I realized that I didn't know any song by memory that I could perform. Barbara noticed my uneasiness, and she handed me a small stack of sheet music.

"Here you go. I have some music right here," Barbara said. "See anything you know?"

I looked through the stack of sheet music and found a popular song by The Carpenters that I had heard many times on the radio.

"*We've Only Just Begun*, I said as I showed her the sheet music. "I know this one."

"Good," she replied as she took the music and placed it on the piano.

I was nervous. Barbara had music, and she was willing to play for me, and it seemed like a safe bet of a song that I could perform, so I figured I had nothing to lose. We began our impromptu rehearsal, and Barbara began the song's introduction. I smiled and listened as she played beautifully. She started her introduction again, and she kept glancing up at me, wondering when I was going to start singing. Nothing. She paused for another moment and went back to playing the introduction once more. I stood there as stiff as a scarecrow in an Arkansas garden. Honestly, I had no clue as to when I was to begin singing along with her. My heart began to race. *Were my brothers right?* I questioned myself. *Maybe I shouldn't be singing in front of an audience!*

"Charles. That was the intro. I'll play the intro, and you come in," she explained kindly.

"Right. The intro."

I didn't know what an intro was. I listened carefully but had no clue when I was to jump in.

"The intro ends here," she pointed, "... and you start."

"Got it. That's the intro," I nodded.

Barbara took another run at it on the piano, and I remained clueless.

"Listen for these two bars," she said as she demonstrated expertly on the piano keys, "and then you come in."

I didn't know a bar from a treble clef sign. I did not know music. In the past, I had only heard music in church and sung along with everyone else. Barbara kept talking about "measures" and "bars" and "keys," and she might as well have been talking to me about one of those farm machines back on the farm I had no clue about.

Finally, the awkward rehearsal in the music building came to a merciful end. I thanked Barbara and left the rehearsal room. I can't imagine what she must have thought of my musical ignorance. As I walked out of the room, I was extremely nervous and questioned my hasty decision to participate. Suddenly, I heard the most beautiful song emanating from another rehearsal room. A piano student was playing it beautifully. The song was the very popular tune "He Touched Me." The composition was written by Bill Gaither and made most famous by Elvis Presley when he used it as his title track on his Grammy Award-winning album.

The beautiful melody consumed me as I walked by. I slowly peered into the room through a small window in the door. I watched the pianist carefully, and I took note of his playing with such concentration and heart. It was as though he really meant what he was playing. A few minutes later, much of my nervousness about the talent show was gone. I walked out of the music building, loving the fact that God had touched me in so many meaningful and significant ways.

That night, I was nervous and excited to stand up in front of hundreds of strangers to perform for the first time at my new school.

"Our next performer is Charles Graham from Dermott, Arkansas," the master of ceremonies announced.

The audience applauded. I stood up from my seat and walked with confidence onto the stage. Barbara played what I considered to be an introduction, and I asked God to help me get through.

"We've only just begun..." I began to sing.

The audience of my new peers listened courteously to the young and naive singer from the South.

"What must they be thinking?" I wondered.

After several measures of singing, we managed to get to the end of the performance. But, rather than leave the stage, I stayed in my place. Sitting near the stage was the piano player I had heard earlier in the rehearsal hall playing "He Touched Me." I looked directly at him and made my request.

"Could you come up here and play for me?"

The students knew that I meant him because I looked him in the eyes. He smiled, and without hesitation he walked up to the stage and to the piano.

"Could you play, *He Touched Me*?" I asked. "I heard you playing it today."

He nodded and smiled, and then started the introduction of the piece. I knew exactly where to come

125

in. Everyone in the room seemed to be familiar with the song. Doug Oldham, The Jordanaires, and many others had recorded *He Touched Me*, but it was Elvis Presley who made Bill Gaither's song popular to the masses.

The song suddenly held a strong and new meaning for me as I stood in front of the student body and shared what had become my testimony. The hand of Jesus had touched me, and no longer would I be the same. As I sang, I looked into many of the eyes of the crowd and noticed that students were wiping tears from their eyes. Some were actually crying. I witnessed firsthand the Holy Spirit moving among boys and girls who also needed the comforting touch of God.

When the song ended, the room was filled with applause, and hearing the applause from the crowd, I felt validated in my singing. Instantly, random students extended invitations to me to sing in their churches. Without hesitation I agreed to go to many new fellowships and sing the one good Christian song I knew—*He Touched Me*.

As the days wore on, I met many more friends, and developing more friendships meant more joy for me. The unforeseen benefit was that my faith began to grow like never before.

CHAPTER 13

"A Season of More Changes"

My first Sunday morning at college, I found myself faced with an unusual quandary. My days in Missouri had already been filled with so many differences compared to my southern Arkansas upbringing, and when Sunday morning arrived, I was forced into another first. All my life I had been programmed to get up on Sunday mornings, put on my Sunday best, and attend our all-black church. Church attendance was not a habit I was going to break just because I was far from home where no one would notice my absence. I was nineteen years old, I was a freshman in college, and I was taking on the world with just Jesus. Church was going to remain a part of who I was.

That first Sunday morning in Bolivar, I stepped out into my new community. I was informed that there was no such thing as a black church in Bolivar, which came as no surprise to me. I didn't have a car, so I had to find a church within walking distance from my dorm. The Southwest Baptist campus sits on hundreds of acres, and simply walking across school property takes a while. Standing on the east side of the student union, I could see in the distance a small church called Southern Hills Baptist. I didn't mind walking to the church. I had done that a lot in my life.

I got out of bed, showered, and put on the only nice suit I had—the black, gray, and white polyester suit I had purchased in Greenville, Mississippi, and had worn to my prom. No, I didn't wear the ruffled shirt or the large burgundy butterfly bowtie that became so popular in the 1970s, but other than that, it looked as if I was ready for a prom date picture that first Sunday. Wearing the eye-catching suit, a white shirt, and a black tie, I entered the church about as inconspicuously as a marching band in the Macy's Thanksgiving Day parade. All eyes were on me.

I was resolved to approach my grand entrance with confidence. Christians were supposed to be welcoming, but I was ready for anything. Thankfully, a male usher dressed in a suit and tie did not ask me to leave or escort me back out the door, instead he just smiled and handed me what the church called a "bulletin." At first I wasn't sure why they gave me the folded piece of paper, but I hung onto it tightly as I walked about two-thirds of the way down the auditorium and found what seemed like the right place to sit. I learned that if I was comfortable, it helped others to be comfortable. I sat with confidence and with an understanding that there was no way my 6'3" frame was going to do anything inconspicuous.

During my phone call to Wanda later that day, I got to explain it all.

"They did what?" Wanda asked in disbelief.

"They gave me a bulletin. It's like a program with a list of everything they were going to do during the service."

"Why?" she asked.

"I guess they don't want any surprises like in our church!" I laughed.

Wanda knew exactly what I meant. At our churches back home, our services could go on and on until the pastor finally closed us in a prayer. We were used to spending two or three hours in our church listening to the pastor.

"Did they stick to the program?"

"They did!"

I went on to explain to my sister just how amazed I was to follow the play-by-play in the program. There was congregational singing, a prayer, a song, announcements, another prayer, an offering, special music, a sermon (that lasted less than forty-five minutes), and a closing prayer. As Reverend Dennis Betts led the service down the pre-planned list in the bulletin, I kept tabs. I told Wanda it was nice, it was orderly, and it was completed in a timely manner.

My biggest impression regarding the day was that the service had a determined ending. The "benediction," as it was called in the bulletin, meant everybody in the church could see the end of the service on the schedule. How refreshing it was to me to be informed as to what was going to happen. And it was great to know that we would be getting out of the morning service long before mid-afternoon.

The service that morning began what I refer to as my cultural stretching. I was beginning a process of learning how other people in places of worship conducted themselves. I will never forget how completely welcomed I felt at the church. It was a little piece of heaven to worship with persons so different, and yet they were so much like me because of the bond of God's love.

This may seem like a strange side-note, but another memory of attending a Baptist college and church far from my home was moments when friends would ask me if I was sure of my salvation. It was a strange question to me. I thought they were implying that I had to be re-baptized. Had they really known what I had gone through regarding my first baptism, they would have understood why I answered the way I did.

"Of course I'm sure!" I would reply to anyone who questioned me.

I later learned that the churches were equipped with beautiful baptisteries full of warm, clear water and a guarantee of no gars.

The college was located in a town where the population was almost one hundred percent white, I didn't fully realize that facet before I settled into my new home. I was naive back then. When I was in the town shopping, people would often ask if I played basketball. I used to think it was because I was quite a bit taller than my friends. It did not occur to me until much later that they were asking the question because I was black. I didn't realize that the dorm mom's effort to place me on the wing with the basketball players as the school's attempt to keep all the black students together.

I made the choice to not let that fact discourage me. I just accepted that I was part of a very small ethnic minority and went about my business of being a student.

I have always been and will always be a people person, and because I enjoy meeting new people, it helped make my transition into college easier for me. Seeing guys from my dorm as I walked through the halls gave me a sense of community and belonging. I experienced what it felt like to enter a classroom and have my presence immediately change the diversity in the room. Had I entered any room apprehensively, it may have sent a message of timidity and self-doubt to others. As a rule, I've found that walking into any situation with confidence always makes things better.

My freshman year, excitement and confidence shielded me from some of the cultural things that bothered me in the past. There was one humorous event that I must share that had to do with one of my preconceived notions. I was walking through the student union by myself when a sign posted at the entrance of a small prayer chapel caught my attention. Affixed to the wall was a plaque that read, "White Chapel." You can imagine my surprise.

Pausing, I thought, *What do I do with this moment?* I reached for the door handle and opened it to see an empty prayer chapel. Uncertain as to what the repercussions might be, I walked to the front row and took a seat.

Silence.

I waited alone in the quietness of the room. Finally, the door behind me opened, and a young white couple entered. I took a deep breath and thought of what I would say once they said the predictable; *This chapel is for whites only.*

I waited. The sweet young lady and her boyfriend said "hello" and then sat down next to each other in another pew. They held hands and prayed. I just sat there motionless. It was weird. They did not confront me or say a thing about my being in the wrong place. I came to the conclusion that the couple must have been used to people of color in public places. Although there was no confrontation that morning, I still felt challenged by the situation.

"I can't believe the school has a chapel for whites only," I told my roommate when I returned to the dorm.

"What're you talking about?"

"The white chapel in the student union? I saw the sign. I walked in and sat on the front pew anyway."

Suddenly, Jerry burst into laughter. Meanwhile, I sat on my bed, fuming at his insensitivity and lack of understanding. He obviously didn't understand what I was feeling at that moment.

"It's not funny, Jerry."

"Yes, it is, Charles. You're at a college."

"So? What difference does that make?"

"People give money to colleges. Right?"

"Yes. So?"

"When they donate money, they get their names put on the buildings. Just look around."

"You mean ..."

"Yes! Mr. and Mrs. White donated money, so they get their name on the chapel—the chapel that you just protested in," Jerry explained and burst into laughter again.

You can imagine how embarrassed I felt as I had to humble myself and listen to Jerry's uncomfortable truth.

As the first semester flew by, my small world had expanded greatly since high school graduation. My week of final exams came and went, and soon I found myself back on the steps of my old house in Dermott for Christmas break.

"Hey, everybody, Charles is home!"

My brothers and my sisters shouted and jumped around me as we hugged each other.

The familiar chatter of too many people speaking at the same time came rushing back over me, and the feeling of home enveloped me. After a moment, through the crowd of my loving family members I saw my father making his way slowly towards me. His steps were careful, halted and difficult for him since suffering his stroke. It was a difficult moment for me as we stood there looking at each other. He was a shadow of the man of strength I had known as a boy.

With his cane in his hand, he held out his arms, and for the first time in a very long while my father gave me a strong embrace I shall never forget. As I wrapped my arms around him, I felt him cry. Suddenly, all those years of feeling as if my father didn't understand me began to melt away. With that one Christmas homecoming embrace, my father was telling me that he was proud of me and that he loved me. What a gift!

The next few days are a bit blurred now as I remember settling back into the house for the winter break. My old job selling clothing at Abrams was available to me, so I picked up right where I had left off so many months before. Christmas gift-buying was in full swing as customers came in for their last-minute gifts, and I was eager to help make their holiday preparation easier.

A few days into the job and hectic week of pre-Christmas purchases—December eighteenth to be exact—I went to work as usual, and at lunch time I left the store to grab a quick bite to eat. As I walked back into the store, my boss, Mr. Brunner, met me and informed me that my sister had been trying to reach me by telephone. I wasn't sure why Mr. Brunner was so serious, but I could tell by the tone in his voice that something was terribly wrong.

"Charles ..." Mr. Brunner began.

"Yes, sir?"

"It's your father."

"Yes?"

"Your father died, Charles. I'm so sorry."

My body went numb as I stared at Mr. Brunner, trying to accept what I had just heard. I don't remember if anything that he said after that. I turned and walked up the stairs, which led to storage rooms above the store. I had to be alone for a few minutes. On my knees I bowed my face into my hands and prayed.

Lord, I don't know what we will need as a family, but I know we will need You. Please, help us get through this. After composing myself, I walked down the stairs and out the front door of the department store. I quickly made my way back to our house. When I arrived, the atmosphere in the room was understandably sad and heavy. I discovered that my dad had been taken to the hospital, and I also learned that dad had died while my mother was away shopping. Soon, Mother returned from town to find us all at the house waiting for her. My older brother broke the sad news.

Just like that, Dad was gone, and my dear mother was a widow. His sudden passing cast a shadow over that Christmas, and things would never be the same in our home. Christmas and the beginning of a new year with my family in Dermott came and went with a heavy feeling of sadness. My heart broke for my mother, who suddenly had all the responsibility of raising my younger siblings. Despite the weight of her obligations, she encouraged me to stay the course and to finish what I had begun in Missouri. Although I struggled with leaving my mother with the family burden, before long, I was back at Southwest Baptist, continuing my education and pursuing my dreams.

At Southwest Baptist, any student could join the campus choir if they wished. Although I declared art as my major, I was excited to become a member of the choir.

Even with my obvious lack of formal training, I remained focused and determined to make music a part of my life. I continued befriending the music majors and continued to surround myself with musical student friends. I joked that they were paying for their degrees, and I was getting free music tips from them along the way. I may not have had the academic instruction they were getting, but I had the desire in my heart to sing.

Another significant event during my freshman year was when I was introduced to the music and friendship of The Lighthouse Quartet, a singing group of SBU students based out of Mount Vernon, Missouri. Three Campbell brothers, Doug, Darrel, and David, their bass singer, Adrain Lemen, and their bass guitarist, Bob Moses, made up the group. Doug and Darrel lived in my dorm, and they had heard me sing *Battle Hymn of the Republic*. During their concert at Southern Hills, they invited me to join them on stage and sing that song. It's a moment that I will never forget because it helped launch me and define who I was as a musical artist on campus.

The Campbells embraced me as a singer and as a friend. One weekend they took me to their home to meet their parents, Jack and Jo Campbell. Mount Vernon was a small town where the only black person for miles was a gentleman who raised the American flag in front of the post office. He was a military veteran who had found peace and his place in a tiny Southwest Missouri town. What I remember most about my first trip to Mount Vernon was that the people loved me and accepted me without question. People such as the Campbells and the Reverend Hubert Conway family took me in as one of their own. I did not know how broken I was and how much I needed unconditional acceptance until I was embraced by families like the Campbells and Conways.

Each year, students from SBU were provided opportunities to serve as summer missionaries. One of the mission projects was an outreach to under-served kids in New York. When I saw those two words, "New" and "York," my imagination raced. All my life I had heard of the "Big Apple," and there was no way I was passing up my chance to visit the greatest city in the world.

After training in Syracuse, New York, I was assigned to work with Reverend Byron Lutz, the pastor of Fillmore Avenue Baptist Church, Buffalo, New York.

The small Polish community was not the picture I had painted in my mind. I had envisioned working with underprivileged youth in the inner-city boroughs of New York City, but the path God had me on was helping children in rural New York. *This is definitely not New York City,* I wisely concluded as I ended up at Camp Iron Bell, a small camp deep in the woods of a random county. But as I have often learned in my ministry, God takes us to the places He wants to use us, regardless of our preconceived notions. We would minister at Fillmore Avenue Baptist Church in the city on the weekend, and then travel each Monday out to the camp for the week. The campers were poor, and many had no change of clothing and would arrive each day dressed exactly as they were the day before. Before the campers arrived, we purchased new sleeping bags for many of them who had no bedding for their bunks. We also bought toothbrushes and other toiletries they needed.

As I settled in with my fellow missionaries, I wondered what God was up to, having sent me to the remote cornfields near Buffalo instead of the brick and mortar of New York City. I learned, *God will use me wherever I am willing to go.*

It was obvious that some of the farmers in that part of the country were not fond of our bringing inner-city kids out to the camp. While we were taking the campers for a walk one night, someone shot at us. That incident confirmed that some of the locals did not like our presence. Watching God change the lives of those campers that summer made it one I've never forgotten.

One of the stranger stories to come out of my mission trip that summer was when a man stood up and spoke during a youth rally. His life had been transformed by an encounter with Jesus. To my surprise, during his testimonial to the congregation, he admitted that he had seen me in the park one weekend and pointed a gun at me with the intention of *taking me out.* He told us that all his life he had harbored prejudice in his heart. He continued to describe what was happening in the park the day he aimed a gun at me. He said there was a *big guy* standing with me that blocked his aim and kept him from pulling the trigger. On that particular day that he was recounting, I was alone in the park.

Also, while serving the Fillmore Avenue Baptist Church in Buffalo, we were joined by a youth choir from Eastside Baptist Church in Marietta, Georgia, directed by Billy Jack Greene. Along with their concerts, they assisted us with the vacation Bible schools in the local parks. Billy Jack asked if I would perform a song with his choir. I accepted his invitation and was asked to sing a song written by Andre Crouch, entitled, *My Tribute.* I also performed my go-to favorite, *Battle Hymn of the Republic*. At the end of summer, I was invited to join the choir in Georgia for their end-of-tour concert. My summer missionary work that year led to many meaningful and life-long friendships. For instance, one friend, Reid Hall, has produced most of my musical recordings; another friend, Steve Leary, impacted my life because of his unconditional love of the Lord and his love for people. I dedicated one of my albums to him when he passed away.

My sophomore year, a friend invited me to a concert of Christian recording artist and television personality Tom Netherton. The concert was only twenty-five miles from our campus, and I was thrilled to think that I could be so close to a legitimate singing star. As much as I enjoyed his concert, it was the invitation he gave at the end of the night that challenged me to consider living a more devoted life for Christ.

"Some of you are being called to full-time Christian service," Tom told the audience.

He said if we were feeling a tug at our hearts, it could be an indication that we were being asked by God to surrender our lives into full-time Christian service. I wanted to go forward, but I was unable to move. I gripped the back of the pew in front of me, and for some inexplicable reason I could not step out of the pew and walk down the aisle that evening.

Back at the campus, my mind had been doing battle for several hours. I was either going to give in to the prompting of the Holy Spirit, or I was going to ignore and reject His urging. About two o'clock in the morning, I wandered around the campus and prayed the prayer that changed my life.

Please, Lord, I will surrender to full-time Christian service. I ask You to help me make it always about You, and not about me. I give you that place in my life.

Today, I still double-check my motives for what I am doing regarding ministry. God will often remind me not to get ahead of Him.

The Baptist Student Union sponsored me in a concert held in the gymnasium. Songwriter and arranger Jerry Estes, a fellow student, graciously agreed to accompany me. With Jerry's capable artistry on the keys and a microphone in my hand, I belted out my tried-and-true songs that were helping me through revivals and mission trip rallies. I wished that my family could have been there; what a blessing it was. I discovered later that somebody in the audience had recorded my premiere concert. After hearing that recording, all I can say is God must have really blessed the audience's ears.

I have since developed a greater appreciation for what God did for me regarding my music development. It was a humble beginning when I was living in our crowded little house on the farm. I saved my money, and I purchased a tiny transistor radio that I kept near my bed. I remember standing at Morgan and Lindsay's store, feasting my eyes on that little source of musical joy. The body of the radio was silver, and it was protected by a red leather case. On its top it had an antenna that telescoped out for better reception. I had to have it. I paid my money, and I bought a battery so I could hurry home and listen to it.

At home, I held that radio in my hand as if it were gold. I switched it on and turned the small dial on the side, trying desperately to tune in a clear radio station. I can't say I preferred country music, but I hated static, and the only station that came in crystal clear was KVSA, a country music station. I learned to love the smooth musical styling of singers such as Conway Twitty and Johnny Cash. My first concert at Southwest Baptist was far from the professionalism of a Twitty or Cash. Everyone has to start somewhere, and for me, it was at SBU that night.

During my sophomore year, my friend Jim and I decided it would be great to have a place off campus that we could rent and call our own. At SBU, there was still a policy that freshman students had to live on campus, but I felt it was time to get out of the noisy dorms and into a rental near the college campus.

"My parents got a call from the school today," Jim revealed to me.

"About what? Is everything okay?" I asked.

"Someone in the administration wanted to know if my parents were aware that I intended to rent a place with you. They talked to my dad about it," Jim said.

He didn't have to tell me. It was obvious that his father, a pastor, had been informed that his son was about to share an apartment with a black student.

"What did your dad say?" I asked.

Jim just smiled and said, "My dad asked them if they had called your parents, too."

It was moments like that, which helped me become closer to friends like Jim. His father demonstrated in one sentence that he was not a prejudiced man; while at the same time he illuminated the fact that the school should check its motives. It was a bonding moment for Jim and me.

On a side note, as Jim and I found advertisements in the newspaper regarding apartments for rent, Jim would call to see if the apartment was available. If it was still for rent, we would get in his car and hustle over to the place to check it out. On several occasions, he was told that the apartment was available, but strangely, by the time the landlord saw the two of us, we would be given the news that we were too late.

"I'm sorry. The apartment was just rented," the man informed us.

"But you just said on the telephone it was available," Jim protested.

The door would close, and Jim and I knew that they were never going to rent their apartment to a black person. After weeks of looking, we were finally able to rent a trailer just off campus.

Another awkward moment that year happened the first day I went to my math class. I enrolled late, and when I arrived to the crowded classroom, it was packed with students sitting in their respective seats.

As I entered the room, I thought of the term *sticking out like a sore thumb.* In my case, I was standing in a room with no place to sit. The professor looked at me, and I looked at him.

"Just a second," the teacher said as he exited the room.

I watched as the professor positioned a desk and chair in the hallway. He told me that the chair positioned just outside the doorway would be where I would sit. Like an elementary child being banished to the hall for disrupting class, I walked out of the room and sat in the hall. I listened to the lecture through the doorway. I would like to say that only happened that day and that there was a desk placed in the room for me the next time class rolled around, but in fact, I spent much of the semester out in the hall. It was not the entire semester, but it felt like it. I have since talked to my former professor about that situation, and I learned that it disturbed him much more than it did me.

Despite those kinds of incidents and moments of insensitivity, I still have very fond memories of my time at Southwest Baptist University. I'm happy to say that the community has grown and evolved since my time there. The university is full of diversity, and I would recommend it to anyone wishing to further his or her education on a Christian campus.

Southwest Baptist College, (later renamed Southwest Baptist University) is where so many firsts happened for me. It's where my music ministry was launched and where I first traveled with friends and ministered in revivals. Those were lean times for as we pinched our pennies to make it through college. We rode in the same car, and we stayed in the same cheap hotel rooms. I'm sure we seemed really youthful and inexperienced, however, we learned to allow the Holy Spirit to lead us and develop us as ministers.

After one of the services, I was invited to go to a home where the youth were gathered. We played games and had a lot of fun. Over the years, I've been blessed to meet youth pastors, music ministers, and preachers who have a zeal for the Lord and genuinely loved people.

After my first revival I was surprised when the preacher, a fellow student, handed me a check for thirty dollars.

"What's this for?" I asked.

"It's for singing during the revival," he explained.

"Wow! Praise the Lord," I replied.

I went to the revival and sang my heart out, but I did not expect to get paid for praising Jesus. I was so privileged to be there and to have the chance to make friends and see the Holy Spirit move in lives. I had no idea I would be getting paid for singing in church.

CHAPTER 14

"Turning the Page"

For many reasons, I don't think I was college material. Yes, I was attending college, but staying at SBU or any college wasn't where I truly wanted to be. I wanted to be out in the world singing and getting my life and my ministry started. I struggled with the thought of whether I should stay in school or leave. I also struggled with how I could possibly tell my family if I quit school. They were so proud of my stepping out and leaving our little town in Arkansas to pursue a degree and a dream. They were so excited to see the first Graham accepted into an institution of higher learning. It had never been done in the history of my family and I could not bear the thought of disappointing my siblings and my mother. I desperately wanted to tell my family that I was quitting -- I just couldn't. Not yet.

One of my good friends, Greg Fiebig, informed me that after he graduated SBU it was his intention to go to Central Missouri State University to earn his masters degree in theater. As we talked about his future, it was the first time I had ever heard of CMSU, but suddenly it felt like if I transferred there with Greg it would be a natural escape hatch. Also, one of the first friends I made my freshman year in Bolivar was Dave Neuhart, a member of the SBU tennis team. He told me he was going to transfer to that university as well. I thought it was much more than a coincidence when he told me that he was moving to Warrensburg to finish his degree. His parents had recently moved there and accepted teaching positions with the university.

Although I didn't know a thing about Central Missouri State University other than I had two good friends attending there, it really didn't matter. A lateral move to another university would be a step toward leaving college as opposed to telling my mother and family that I was exiting college all together. The truth is I felt it was easier to tell my family that I had transferred to another university than tell them that I had quit school.

Central Missouri State University is located about one hour away from Kansas City, Missouri. Clearly, there were big differences between Southwest Baptist College, a Christian institution, and Central Missouri State University, a much larger state university.

My dorm, however, was a lot like Southwest Baptist in that I got to know my dorm mates immediately. I also found it comforting that Greg, a close friend, would be my roommate. But, getting to know more friends among the several thousand students moving about the new campus was a challenge. At that time in my Christian journey, I was hypersensitive to who might be and who might not be a Christian living around me. I had been very sheltered growing up in Arkansas and I had remained sheltered for two awesome years as I attended a Christian campus in Bolivar. The fact that we only had 1,500 students on the entire SBU campus also made it easier to get to know one another. At Central Missouri, I was suddenly thrust into adjusting to thousands of students from all walks of life and religious beliefs.

I will never forget trying to make quick determinations as to which guys in the dorm might be like-minded and might have a relationship with Jesus.

When we moved into our dorm room I peeked into the next room to see if I could find any indication of what kinds of lifestyles our new suitemates were living. About that time, one of them walked in with what looked like a can of beer in one hand. He took a swig and I immediately thought, *Well that guy is probably an alcoholic and party guy—definitely not a believer. The guy drinks beer!*

I love how God has a sense of humor and how He uses judgmental incidents such as that as teaching moments. "Rondo" was a citrus drink with some national popularity in the late 1970's and early 1980's. If you don't believe me, you can find a goofy old commercial about Rondo on Youtube. The can was obviously designed to look a little like a beer can. It turned out that my suitemate wasn't a drinker at all. In fact, my new next-door neighbor, Bob, came from a Christian family full of blue grass musicians and singers. Bob and his family are dear friends of mine to this day.

One morning, I decided to break as much of the ice between the other students and myself as possible. I made the decision that I would do it by saying "hello" to every student I passed on the sidewalks or in the hallways as I walked to and from class.

"Hello. Good morning. Hi. Hello, there," I said as I met one person, and then another.

How funny it was to see people turn quickly from their sour or pensive attitude, to a smile and a friendly greeting after their initial startled reaction.

"Good morning. Hello," they replied.

It was gratifying to see how that simple greeting broke down so many walls and in a very short amount of time. For me, it was just a matter of being out-going and friendly. When Jesus Christ is in your heart, there should be a constant feeling of joy. Also, I figured when Jesus walked the Earth, He acknowledged those around him. If I was going to be a light and reflection of who He is, I had to be open to all the people on campus.

While a student at Warrensburg, I got a job working as a salesperson at Russell Brothers Clothing Store. The job provided me many opportunities to meet the citizens of Warrensburg. Assisting people in the store ran the gamut of students needing prom clothes to men needing their first suits for funerals or weddings. One encounter I recall was when a mother came in the store needing a belt for her young son, David. Who would have thought that selling a belt would turn into a life-long friendship with David's family? Years after leaving Warrensburg I would periodically drop by their home just to say hello. My friendship with Charles, Lucille, David, Susan, Lucy and Michael, and their dog Ky is still a part of my life to this day. I enjoyed meeting people of the community and being a part of the local ministry in Warrensburg. Being involved in the town, led to opportunities for me to sing in several local churches.

At CMSU, I placed myself right back on the academic track to a degree in graphic design. Since my childhood, drawing and creating art was a natural thing to do, and it was where I found so much peace and creative release. My Mom and my siblings agreed that art was where my gifting was, and their encouragement pushed me to keep pursuing that degree. However, my heart was still in music. One night, I was blessed to perform on campus in front of a large crowd of students of different beliefs. The concert was held at Grinstead Hall and students from all Protestant denominations, the Catholic students, and many un-churched and non-believers from Ellis Hall dormitory came to support me. Opportunities such as that concert placed my spiritual testimony front and center at CMSU.

My faith in God was on display and put into motion in ways I had never anticipated before transferring to the state university. For instance, the night a student on drugs walked into my dorm room to tell me he thought he was dying. With desperation in his voice, he said he needed me to pray with him. As we left my room he picked up my Bible and then continued to his room where we prayed. After some time spent in prayer, he calmed down.

The next morning, he was embarrassed by his actions. He apologized for whatever he had said and done and he told me he was sorry for bringing his troubles to me. I told him no apology was needed, and I quickly assured him that regardless of his trials, I would be there for him. He didn't understand that I had dedicated my life to ministry, no matter what form it took.

On a lighter note, I added to my reputation at CMSU when I became the switchboard operator. My role was to simply answer calls and then connect the caller to their desired party. With that much control at my fingertips, I couldn't help but be a bit mischievous. Guys would call wanting to reach the girls dorm and I could not resist connecting them into "dial-a-prayer." Truth be told, I was a bit like comedienne Lily Tomlin's "Earnestine" character when it came to operating a switchboard. For my younger readers, you can find clips of Earnestine on Youtube. Just search for the TV show, "Rowan and Martin's Laugh In."

Although my year at CMSU was filled with learning new things, accomplishing academic goals, and making many life-long friends, I still felt that being in college was not where I was supposed to be. So, I finally made the decision that I probably should have made the year before, I left college and moved to Independence, Missouri.

The reason I was drawn to Independence was because my friend from SBU, Wes Hazelrigg, lived there. When my father passed away in the middle of my freshman year in college, his death left a huge hole in my life. Wes had introduced me to his amazing family, and their acceptance of me gave me comfort. His father, Delmar, made an immediate impression on me because he had qualities about him that reminded me of my dad. He was a hard worker, a smart man like my father, and he was always happy to share fatherly advice with me.

"It costs just as much to keep your car full of gas as it does to run out," Pop Hazelrigg used to say.

"Yes, sir. Good advice."

In fact, every time I have run out of gas while driving, I can hear Pop's voice. I wish I had taken his advice more to heart.

The Hazelrigg family didn't have to adopt me into their family, but they did. Pop was a man's man and I became his "adopted" son. Pop watched over my financial affairs and he made sure that they were carefully managed. His wife, Ila, watched out for my sweet tooth, and when she heard I was coming to visit she would make the most delicious paradise pie. Paradise pie is an incredible combination of pineapples, sugary stuff, and graham cracker crust.

While writing this book, I received news that Pop was very ill. It was such a privilege to visit him and to let him know how thankful to God I was for his being in my life. Shortly after my visit, I got the inevitable call that Pop had gone home to be with the Lord. Today, I rest in the fact that my adopted dad is rejoicing with the Savior now and some day he and I will be reunited.

When I moved to Independence, Missouri I joined the Immanuel Baptist Church, where Harry Clifton was pastor. Brother Harry and his wife Fern were two of the most gracious people I had ever met. For instance, if Brother Harry were engaged in a conversation with me while surrounded by a crowd of people, he would give me his undivided attention. It was a natural response to Pastor Harry's warm personality to want to become a member of his wonderful congregation. Because I was made to feel so at ease and welcome there, I never second-guessed my desire to join the membership role. My being black in the all white church was never an issue.

With Brother Harry's living example, I learned so much about what a minister should be, and how he or she should treat the persons they serve. As long as I have known him, I have never heard a single bad word said about him.

There was a student choir from Dermott I had invited to perform at Immanuel Baptist the first summer I was a member. The students from my old hometown needed a place to stay, and I helped make the church aware of the need. The choir, made up of black students, had never been in a white church before, and they had never stayed in homes of white families. It was quite a cultural shock for them.

Miss Helen Adams, one of the oldest members of our church, was one of the first to open her home. I was so proud of my church family when many of them opened their homes to host the Dermott choir.

Another music and drama team from Florida made up of young adults came to perform at Immanuel Baptist Church. At the end of their performance, the team invited anyone interested in joining their ministry team to audition. As they shared the truth of the gospel using skits and music, I envisioned myself becoming a part of something exciting.

I auditioned that night, and a few days later I was informed that I had been accepted. Soon, I was on my way to Lake Wales, Florida, to join the group for rehearsals. We spent the summer rehearsing, and then we set out in the fall to begin our performance tour around the United States. Just as I had hoped, the other singers, actors, and crew in the ministry became instant friends.

We traveled from town-to-town fulfilling another dream of mine, which was to see more of the world. It was wonderful to enter different church fellowships and see the new faces every night. There were those who probably heard the good news of Jesus Christ for the first time, simply because it was being delivered in such a unique way.

As I recollect my time with the drama group, I can't in good conscience leave the reader with the impression that everything connected with that experience was completely positive. I would be remiss in not sharing the downside of the experience because it is in the uncertain and uncomfortable times of life that my faith is stretched. It's not because I wish to cast a negative shadow upon the people or the ministry, but this book is an attempt to be transparent and honest about my life and spiritual growth.

One day, before traveling out to minister, one of the directors gathered all the performers.

"We have a problem," she said as she looked around the room.

None of us liked a meeting that started with those words.

"The church where we are to perform next found out that we have a black performer in the group, and they have informed us that we cannot minister in their fellowship," she informed us.

Hearing the announcement came as no surprise. With the welfare of the performers in mind, I spoke up.

"I don't have to go," I said.

"No way! If Charles doesn't perform, neither do we," the group responded as they came to my defense.

The team was sensitive to my journey, and they believed that there was a lot of work to do to bring more awareness to race relations and equality. They were ready to take a stand. And then, it happened.

"Now, hold on." she interrupted. "Let's think this through. This is a big church that you're suggesting I cancel."

Around the room all eyes were shifting from our ministry leader back to me.

I looked into the faces of the other performers and they were obviously stunned at her remarks. Their expressions spoke volumes. *Did she really just suggest we go on without Charles?*

I knew the best solution would be to stay at the ministry base and join them for the next performance. As much as I tried not to let it affect me, I was crushed.

On another occasion, the ministry team was treated to a pool party where hamburgers and hotdogs were served. We were all excited to enjoy each other's company before the teams were divided into three different tour groups to go our separate ways. Although I had experienced a few challenges during the rehearsal months, the challenge that confronted me at the swimming pool that day was one that broke my heart.

The party was over and we were putting things away. On our way back and forth from the kitchen I noticed three young boys standing near the wall that surrounded the pool. Rather than throwing away the leftover hotdogs, I decided to give them to the hungry boys. The director saw what I was doing and immediately walked over to us. He took the hotdogs from the boys and threw the hotdogs on the ground. I was stunned. I looked at him and I looked at the boys. I was so hurt that all I knew to do was go upstairs to my room, pack my luggage, and leave.

The director must have known something was wrong because he sent my good friend to the room to talk to me. I told my friend there was no way I was staying under the circumstances. My mind was made up and I was leaving. He asked if I would talk to the director, but I told him there was nothing the director could say that would change my mind. He pressed me again to talk things over with the director of the ministry. Reluctantly, I agreed. As I continued packing my belongings to leave, the director walked into my room. He asked why I was leaving and I recounted the incident with the three boys by the pool. His response made no sense, and there was no Christian compassion in what he said.

"If we would have fed those three boys, we would have had to feed the entire community," he told me.

"The whole community wasn't standing there. It was just three hungry little boys," I replied.

He agreed that he had made a mistake, and then he asked if I would forgive him. I felt in my heart that I should, so I did. In spite of the many difficulties, God continued to show me that he was in still in control of my life.

After completing my ministry time in Florida, I moved back to the Kansas City, Missouri area. Once again I returned to retail clothing sales working at Jones Store Company. It was during this time I received an invitation to attend a graduation. It came from my friend, Tim, one of the former members of the drama team. I traveled to Adrian, Michigan, where I stayed with Tim and his family. While I was there, Tim's mother asked me to sing during a church revival meeting. That night I sang *We Shall Behold Him*. Afterwards the couple from Tulsa, Oklahoma who had ministered asked if they could pray for me.

The next day the ministers were invited to lunch at Tim's home. At this time in my life I was travelling full-time and getting a good taste of what ministry on the road was like. However, there was one thing that was troubling me as I stepped out into ministry. At SBU I was an art major, not a Bible major, so I felt a little inadequate when it came time to minister. I had become very comfortable singing and performing music, but I lacked confidence when it came to biblical knowledge. So, with that concern in my mind, I seriously considered going to a Bible school in order to minister more effectively. While having lunch with the ministers, they inquired about my plans and asked if I had ever considered attending Rhema Bible Training Center in Tulsa, Oklahoma. Although I had not heard of the school, I could tell by their enthusiasm that they were very anxious to tell me all about it.

"In a few weeks the school will be hosting a camp meeting. We would like for you to be our guest," they informed me.

The ministers were graduates, and they were obviously very familiar with the school and its reputation for preparing students for ministry. As July approached that summer, they wanted me to attend a camp meeting scheduled in Tulsa. When they asked if I could go my calendar wasn't open due to ministry I had booked in Michigan. However, the Michigan opportunity unexpectedly changed and the dates opened back up for my availability in Oklahoma. It was as if I was supposed to be in Tulsa after all. Following God's prompting, I drove my trusty old van, "Nicodemus," all the way to Tulsa and I was determined to discover what a camp meeting was all about.

Although I had never been, I knew that a charismatic camp meeting was going to be a different experience compared to the church meetings I had been a part of to that point. In case I felt uncomfortable during the meeting, I purposely sat in the highest section of the auditorium. No one, but the usher who seated me, seemed to notice that I was attempting to find a good place to be inconspicuous. I listened carefully to excellent Bible teaching, and I found myself really enjoying the service. Still, I was wishing that it were a Baptist school. I assumed that no one in the meeting would understand where I was coming from as a Baptist. We broke for lunch and as that thought consumed me, around the corner walked a couple from my Baptist church in Independence, Missouri. I couldn't believe my eyes.

Just like that, God sent to me Jerry and Shirlene, people I knew and who understood exactly what I was thinking. After a tearful reunion, they invited me to lunch. I couldn't get over how amazing it was that out of the thousands of people I could have bumped into, God sent those two wonderful saints to cross my path. I love when God shows up in loving ways like that.

After lunch, I met with the minister friends who had invited me to the event. They informed me that all the available space in their home had been filled, but they had arranged for me to stay with a young man they knew. Remarkably, they introduced me to the same usher who had seated me earlier in the auditorium.

Time passed, and one day the idea of attending Rhema Bible School was lying so heavy on my heart, it was beginning to consume my thoughts. My original dream while in high school was to study in the city of Tulsa, and attend Oral Roberts University. It was intriguing to ponder going back to Tulsa to study at a Bible college near Oral Roberts. I knew if God wanted me there, my focus would be on spiritual growth and spiritual education, twenty-four seven.

I was reminded that God had a specific plan for my life. Amazingly, the young man who ushered me to my seat, Joe DeAngelo, would become my roommate for the next two and a half years. A meaningful friendship grew between Joe and me at Rhema and later on, I would sing in Joe's wedding, minister in his church, and watch his kids grow up.

I had a place to live, and a direction to go. The next thing on my list was to secure a job. While browsing through the newspaper I saw a job listing for a sales person, but when I walked through the front doors of Drysdales Western Wear, I suddenly felt out of place. As I looked around I made my way to the blue jeans section at the back of the store. The salesperson approached me.

"Are you from around here?" he asked.

"No."

"What brings you to Tulsa?"

"Bible School."

"Which one?"

"Rhema Bible School," I replied.

"Praise God! I go there too!"

That's when I confessed that I was actually there to apply for a job. I asked him for directions to the office, and he was eager to help.

"Go out the front door. Make a left." He replied and then stopped abruptly. "No. Never mind, follow me."

He started walking and led me through the storage room, and then into the office area where he introduced me to the secretary. I thanked him and he returned to the sales floor. I was given an application to fill in, and when I had completed it and handed it back to the secretary, I thanked her and I went back into the store the way I had come in. I walked back to the jeans department to thank Don, the salesmen, for being so helpful. We talked for a moment, until the telephone rang. Don answered the phone and it was the secretary I had met a few minutes earlier. She asked Don if he knew the young man he had ushered back to the office.

"I sure do know him. He's my brother," he laughed.

"Send him back. The manager wants to interview him for the job," she informed him.

"Will do."

I could tell Don was talking about me by the way he kept looking at me during the call.

"Charles, the manager wants to interview you right now. Go on back in there," Don encouraged me.

Without hesitation, I walked back to the manager's office, interviewed for the sales position, and I was hired on the spot. The next day, I was out on the sales floor working for Drysdales Western Wear. I worked the job for two years as I attended school at Rhema. Just as I had done in Missouri, I took time to minister to and develop friendships with my co-workers and management. Many of those relationships still exist today. Mrs. Dry, the owner of the store, asked me to sing a concert for the employees and their families right there in the store.

At Rhema, I learned the value of relationships. It was there I met and befriended Donna Douglass who played Ellie Mae on the TV show, *The Beverly Hillbillies*. The friends I made during my time at Rhema are too many to count, and many of those friends made during my Bible training days are still close friends today. Looking back from this perspective, I think about how everything I experienced helped me in ministry. Some of the lessons I've learned came through heartache, while others were revealed in gentle and humorous ways.

For instance, I have had a long running challenge with sound engineers in churches. I think I will simply refer to them as "sound guys" so as not to offend my engineer friends. In their defense, I will say that many of the men and women who have sat in the back of the auditoriums functioning as sound guys and sound girls have been well intentioned. But every once in a while, there will be someone behind the sound console with little knowledge of how a music concert or service should be conducted, and therefore they are apt to make unexpected choices.

During my early performances, I was accompanied by audiocassettes. Those days were long before CDs, MP3s, or Bluetooth capabilities, which have certainly made my life and the continuity of my performances much more predictable. Unfortunately, there were times when sound engineers took it upon themselves to help me.

One particular Sunday morning, I walked into a church in St. Louis carrying about a dozen cassette soundtracks. I carefully worked out the order in which I wanted to perform the songs, and I cued each song perfectly on each performance tape. I walked into the church sanctuary and handed the cassettes to an elderly fellow who was in charge of all things having to do with the sounds system. Before the congregation entered, I stood on stage and moved carefully through a sound check to determine where the volume settings should be. A few minutes later, people filed into the room and I was blessed to spend some time in prayer with the ministers before the concert.

The church was packed as I introduced myself and welcomed everyone to the church.

"I am so glad to be in the Lord's house with you this evening," I smiled.

Remember, this was in the beginning of my singing ministry when performing was still very new. It was a time when I approached a singing concert with as much planning as I could muster. It had to be right. I had to be as perfect as possible. The faces of the audience were full of anticipation as I gave the soundman a gentle nod and smile:

"My brother; if you would please," I asked politely.

The musical introduction of the first song, *Blessed Assurance*, began. I took a deep breath, and I quietly thanked Jesus for the opportunity to sing his praises.

"Blessed assurance, Jesus is…" I sang.

To my surprise, as I began to sing the song, there was another voice coming out of the speakers with me. The soundman was playing what is called a "demo" track, or demonstration track. That simply means that a recording artist had sung on the first track to give a performer like myself an example to follow. After the performance track, there was a silent space on the tape, and then the following track would be the instrumentals with no voice. That's the track I needed but had not received from the well-meaning soundman.

I laughed and informed the audience, "That guy is a good singer, but I didn't come here to do a duet."

There must have been some people in the congregation who had some music and technology knowledge because I saw a few folks smiling along with me. But for the most part, I would say the congregation was unaware of what was really happening.

Amazingly, the soundman kept the track with the singer going, as if that was the way the concert was supposed to be. I stopped singing and gently indicated to the soundman that he had started the wrong track.

"If you could, my brother, please fast-forward the tape to the performance track," I requested with a kind smile.

The sound guy tilted his head as if to say he didn't understand the problem.

"My brother, that's the wrong track. Fast-forward the tape, if you would, please?"

He played the music over the speakers as the congregation waited patiently and I listened carefully for the cue.

"Keep going," I coached.

He pushed "play" and the tape was almost to the end.

"Keep going," I encouraged with a smile.

Unfortunately for everyone in the room, he fast-forwarded the tape a bit too far.

"Go back a little, my brother," I suggested. "A little more. More. A bit more."

The well-meaning brother finally found the beginning of the song and I jumped in. We successfully made it through Blessed Assurance, although I had never sung that song with less assurance.

When the song ended, I requested he put in the next cassette. That was the moment that the congregation and I found out the scope of what had happened before my concert. The soundman began the next tape and Sandy Patty's voice beautifully filled the room with mine. Suddenly, Sandy and I were singing our first and only duet.

"Excuse me, my brother, but the tapes should all be cued to the performance track."

"Okay. I rewound them all," he revealed to me.

161

"Excuse me?" I asked and braced myself for his explanation.

"I had to rewind all of the tapes to the beginning for you," he said. "I'll fast forward them and you tell me when I get close," he smiled.

All thirteen songs were improperly cued and the poor soundman was going to have to fast forward every tape before the congregation could hear me sing each selection. As the concert continued, there were several songs I simply had to jump into at random moments in order to keep the service moving.

A technique I have developed over the years is sharing scripture, or speaking from my heart as the introduction of the song is playing. It is a good way to share and keep the interest of the audience. Unfortunately, that particular soundman was not aware of my technique. As the concert progressed, the music would begin and I would attempt to share my thoughts. Suddenly, the music that was accompanying me would go silent.

I would stop speaking and indicate to the soundman that he should begin again. He would smile and start the music. I started speaking again through the introduction and the music would abruptly stop. At my every attempt to speak, he would stop the music. I finally surrendered to the soundman and kept silent during each song's introduction.

When the unique concert ended, the sweet and oblivious soundman approached me with my box of performance cassettes. He was beaming with so much pride for having assisted me in what he thought was a wonderful concert. All I could do was smile and thank him for his dedicated effort.

Another unpredictable aspect of my ministry is when I wander into the unknown ability of the pianist who has been assigned to play for me. As the visiting minister, I never know what level of talent is coming my way. One pianist I remember fondly was a sweet sister who had been sitting at the church's piano since the 1950s. To give you a point of reference, she had the same seat in her church since the day I was born. Still, I would have to delicately say that her faithfulness had surpassed her ability. When she played, it didn't matter how badly I wished the tempo to be hurried, she could only play it at her familiar slow tempo. All of my smiling and directing her with my hands had no affect upon her tempo. She was content to play nice and slow, the way she had for many decades.

Another part of my music journey I discovered is that there is often a preconceived notion people have of music styles because their notions are based upon the performer's look and attitude. Whether it is hairstyle, body type, skin color, accent, place of birth, clothing … or in my case, ethnicity, people anticipate a certain type of music to be performed based on the externals they see.

Black gospel singers can really sing, Charlie. I know you're going to blow their socks off.

Those kinds of remarks haven't happened solely in the white churches. Black congregations have their established preconceptions as well.

We love gospel music.

Their reference point was probably the songs and styles of the last black performer they heard in their church. At my concerts, the congregation might be set to hear one thing, and I would deliver a sound different than expected, especially if I began the ministry time with a Sandy Patty or Larnelle Harris song.

You didn't sing like we expected. I really liked it.

Those were the kinds of remarks I might hear. Often, people didn't realize how condescending they were being. What congregations didn't know was how hard I had worked to deliver music that God had put in my heart. Making my way into small, rural, white churches helped me understand their point of reference. In many cases, I was not only the first black to minister on their stage, but I was the first black to physically be inside their church!

I have some wonderful friends who live in Jefferson City, Missouri and I have had memorable concerts there. But, one morning while I was visiting I was deeply disappointed. After the concert a young girl came up to me and asked for a moment of my time. I listened carefully as she explained what was troubling her.

"My dad was going to come today. He decided not to."

"What happened?" I asked innocently.

"He heard you would be here."

"Yes?" I asked, encouraging her to continue.

"He said he wouldn't come to church this morning because our church was letting a black man perform on stage."

"Oh. I'm sorry he felt that way," I said disappointedly.

Although I was saddened by what she had revealed to me, I took the opportunity to spend time, minister to her, and discuss God's love.

On another Sunday morning in Missouri, I finished my concert and an elderly man using a walking cane, made his way up to me. Without saying a word, he leaned his cane against a pew, opened his arms, and we shared an embrace. After the hug, he picked up his cane and made his way silently out of the church.

"You'll never know how much that means to me," the man's daughter said. "My father is a very prejudice man."

"You have blessed me," I told her.

With the many difficult and disappointing moments of ministry in the past, it was refreshing to witness such a healing experience.

A few years ago as I was in a southern suburb of Chicago, I sang in a church where the neighborhood had recently undergone a dramatic change. The pastor, a long-time friend of mine, had invited me but he did not tell the congregation that I was black. The pastor knew the presence of God was what was needed in the service and not a description of the invited guest. A woman walked up to me after the service and I could see that she was eager to tell me something.

"I told my husband that I was going to bake a cake and take it to our new black neighbors who moved in next door. My husband and I had quite an argument about it and he demanded that I not take it. I took it anyway, and I found them to be very sweet neighbors. We came to church after the argument, only to find you, a black man standing in our pulpit ready to minister to us. I wasn't sure how the morning was going to end," she explained as they both shook my hand and smiled.

God moved in their hearts that morning in such a way that they have financially supported my ministry down through the years.

I'll wrap up this chapter with another heartwarming story about how God works in the hearts of his people. I ministered for twenty-five years in a youth camp that started in a man's cornfield near Dixon, Illinois. On my way home, I was giving thanks to God for another wonderful camp where lives of young people were changed through salvation. God had given the students purpose and meaning. In the middle of my giving thanks, my van suddenly broke down. I was just north of Peoria, Illinois, and this was a time long before cell phones were invented. After multiple attempts to flag down passing vehicles for help, I was becoming very discouraged.

"Lord, please send me some help. I'm stranded and I'm trying to get home," I prayed.

Just then, a car with an elderly white couple and an older passenger in the back seat pulled off the road. The gentleman at the wheel slowly rolled down his window about an inch. I could see he was very leery of speaking with me, but he felt compelled to be of assistance.

"Need some help?" He asked tentatively.

I could tell that he and his passengers were nervous about stopping to help me. It didn't help that there had been a recent race riot in the Peoria area.

"Oh, praise God you stopped! I'm Charles Graham," I told him.

My words and my demeanor gave the driver some confidence that I was safe to speak with. He introduced himself as Orville, and then he retrieved jumper cables right away from the trunk of his car. Unfortunately, the jumper cables had no affect on my van.

"I'm Orville Schroer. Get in the car and I'll take you to a service station," Orville said.

I got in the back seat of his car with the elderly person and we went to a service station. The passenger in the backseat with me was even older than the senior citizen couple in the front seat.

"Charles, this is my wife, Leone, and that's my mother-in-law," Mr. Schroer said with a smile.

Because it was the Fourth of July weekend, we were greeted with more disappointing news when we arrived at the service station.

"The tow truck won't be available until tomorrow. What hotel are you staying in?" the service station attendant asked.

"He'll be staying with us," my new friend Orville said proudly.

I was humbled by Mr. Schroer's hospitality and courage to take me in during my time of need. He could have easily dropped me off at a hotel and felt satisfied about doing his good deed for the day. At the Schroer's house, Orville, his wife, and his mother-in-law, went into the house as I gathered my luggage from the trunk of his car. When I walked up to the front door and entered, I took the little grandmother by surprise.

"Orville! There's a black man in the house!"

"Yes, Mom. I know. That's Charles. He's staying with us," Orville replied.

Mrs. Schroer showed me to the guest room where I would be staying. Mr. Schroer walked in a few minutes later.

"I have to go a church meeting this evening," he said. "My wife and mother-in-law will be going with me. Here's some money for dinner. Here's an extra key to the house, and a key to our extra car if you need it."

You can imagine how surprised I was to have complete strangers trusting me and giving me gifts after having just met me. They left for their meeting, and I drove down the road to a church I had seen on the way to their home. As I sat in church, I felt so humbled and thankful to God for attending to every detail of my need. I prayed that God would bless Mr. and Mrs. Schroer for the charity they had shown to a complete stranger.

Although I had a lot on my mind regarding my broken-down vehicle and ministry, I rested well that night in their guest room. The next morning, I walked into the kitchen to find that Mrs. Schroer had breakfast ready for me.

"Good morning, Charles," she said.

"Good morning," I replied as I looked for her husband to walk in.

"Orville has left," she informed me.

"Oh. I'm sorry I missed him."

"He'll be back. He's taking care of your truck. He had it towed and they are getting it fixed for you."

"He didn't have to do that."

"You have a seat and enjoy some breakfast," Mrs. Schroer instructed as she served me.

"You have been so kind to me. Thank you so much."

"Before we saw you on the side of the road yesterday, Orville and I had been talking about getting out of the ministry. Before going to bed last night, we talked about the things you shared with us regarding your ministry and how God is directing you. Listening to you helped us realize that we can't quit. Our church is struggling and we have been wondering if it is our time to go. You'll never know how much you have encouraged us to keep going,"

When I left Dermott, Arkansas, I left with the dream and vision that God had placed in my heart. It was a script that I would have never written for myself as I continued experiencing the beautiful humanity of Christian brothers and sisters across America. Doing my ministry on weekends in the United States was just the beginning of what has become a life long trek serving my King. The apostle Paul referred to a life serving Jesus as a race to be run. In May of 1984, I graduated from Rhema Bible College with a feeling that I was much more prepared to continue running my personal race. I was more confident as I followed my calling. A few months after graduation, the race officially took on an international scope.

CHAPTER 15

"Go Into All the World"

SOUTH AMERICA

When I think back to when my international travels began, I think of my trip to Columbia, South America. I was invited by Reverend Bob Shrimpton to join their Fee Fee Baptist Church mission team in Saint Louis, Missouri. The Shrimpton's daughter and son-in-law, Linda and Ron Springgate, worked in Columbia as foreign missionaries.

Again, I realized how God orchestrates his plans for my life. In this instance, a simple friendship from college turned into the key reason for my first mission trip beyond the borders of the United States. What a thrill it was to secure my first passport, which would give me access to travel the world. I was living in Tulsa as I filled in all the paperwork and received my passport. With that document in hand, I gassed up old "Nicodemus." Why that name for my van? I named my van Nicodemus after the biblical character who met Jesus at night. The old van had no air conditioning, which meant traveling at night was much more comfortable.

I headed to Saint Louis to rendezvous with the Shrimptons and their mission team. Before long, I was boarding an airplane at Lambert International Airport in Saint Louis, and we were on our way to Bogotá, Columbia in South America. It was the beginning of many ministry flights to come.

While in Columbia, our mission team worked in Bogota, Cartagena, and Barranquilla helping to educate pastors and other missionaries from all over Columbia and surrounding countries. We attended missionary conferences, which were very encouraging and educational for the dedicated men and women of South America. My role with the mission team was to minister to the children of missionaries. As their parents met daily at the conference, I worked with other missionaries conducting Bible studies, teaching music, and producing drama. I encouraged the students to tell me their stories of what it was like to have parents as missionaries. The children adapted their personal stories into a dramatic presentation that proved to be enlightening for all of us, especially to their parents

Our technique was to use drama to encourage the students to open up about what it was like to follow their parents onto the mission field. I figured the parent's decision to answer the call to go into missions could be difficult for the children. I wanted the students to find the joy in the journey that God had prepared for them as children of missionaries. In the dramatic presentation, the students communicated what they enjoyed about their life, and they shared the challenges they faced that most kids would never have to endure. They told stories of going back to the United States and other children making fun of them. They were call names like, "jungle bunnies" because their peers in their home state pictured missionaries living in the jungles with the natives.

Once the script was completed, we assigned the student actors the characters they would portray. As they acted out their stories, their parents and the audience gained new insight as to some of the things the children were dealing with. Some of the hardest things we heard were how the children didn't feel like they belonged, whether on the mission field or back in their home country. They were weary from having to defend themselves against stereotypes.

I felt that our purpose was to help the students understand that God would not place such a call on their parents without equipping them as well. The presentation had quite the impact and I still receive Christmas cards from some of the men and women who were children in that drama. Some of the children have even become missionaries like their parents.

During my time in Columbia, I tagged along with some of the medical personnel to observe them, and to help them as needed. When we visited villages and poor parts of the cities, I saw firsthand extreme poverty and despair. I always thought that my family and I were poor because we had holes in the roof, and no running water. But, when I saw the living conditions of hundreds of men, women and children living in tiny shelters made of cardboard or tin, I witnessed what real poverty looked like. The sad look on their faces has stayed in my mind ever since. That experience made me grateful to God for the simple wooden house where I was raised.

Later, we ventured outside the cities and into the countryside to minister to people. Columbia is a country full of mountains, streams, waterfalls, and incredibly beautiful flowers growing everywhere. But after seeing the faces of the struggling people who inhabit much of the country, my mind wouldn't allow me to fully enjoy the scenery. All I could see was the sad eyes of the children, and ponder their tremendous needs.

One day, I sat next to a man on a bench and I attempted to share my faith with him. He was trying his best to communicate with me, and I was doing my best to understand and communicate back to him using hand signals and speaking what Spanish I could muster. I would gesture and describe to him how I had flown on an airplane to get to Columbia. He would gesture back and speak fluent Spanish, but I couldn't figure out what he was trying to get me to understand!

Despite our struggles, we both had a desperate desire to break through the barriers and find some understanding. By the end of the week, God knitted our hearts together as we used translators to share our stories. I was able to share my faith with him, and by the end of the week, my new friend had made a commitment to Christ. After I returned to the United States, he and I kept in touch for a while.

Just outside the conference center where we were staying, was the bustling city of Bogotá. My missionary friends had two young children, Amy and Shelley, who would escort me down the street to a nearby store where we would buy Coca Cola. The children could speak Spanish to the man behind the counter and tell him what we wanted to purchase. A few days later, I had enough confidence to step out on my own and walk into the store for a Coke. I had it all planned and I even carried the exact amount of change in my pocket to make the transaction simple. But when I walked into the store, and I asked the owner for a Coke, he said, *No Coke*, and then he continued speaking more Spanish.

Suddenly, all my confidence evaporated. I felt like a lost foreigner in a foreign land. I smiled, turned around and walked swiftly back to the conference center never to venture out again without my translators.

One trip that made up for my Coca Cola buying failure, was when Amy and Shelley took me to a shopping center so I could buy some gifts to take back to America. I told the girls to tell the sales ladies that we were "just looking" and that we didn't need their assistance. I watched as the girls communicated to the women, and then I noticed the ladies whispering to each other. I could tell their giggles and chatter was directed toward me.

"What are they saying?" I asked the girls.

"We can't say, Uncle Charles," they told me.

"Come on. Are they talking about me?" I pressed.

"We can't tell you."

The girls and I finished our shopping and we left the store. I pressured them even more to tell me what the sales ladies had been whispering. Finally, the missionary girls revealed their secret.

"They thought you were very handsome and cute, Uncle Charles!" they laughed.

THE UNITED KINGDOM

In 1984, I was a student at Rhema in Tulsa. I was privileged to sing at the beginning of a conference at our school one Sunday morning, but by Wednesday, I was sick and I didn't even get out of bed to go to class.

Lying in bed, I remembered a lesson I heard earlier in the week based on Hebrews 11:1: *Now faith is the substance of things hoped for and the evidence of things not seen.*

The teacher had emphasized the word, "Now" as he taught the verse. He asked us to consider the word, "now." *What would you do if what you were believing for was already done?*

I asked myself that question, and because I truly believed I was already healed, I got out of bed and attended the conference. The crowded conference had already begun when the usher led me down to one empty seat. When I sat down, the person next to me asked:

"Aren't you the young man who sang so beautifully on Sunday?" the man said in his British accent.

"Yes," I replied.

He smiled to his wife, and we settled in to listen to the conference speaker. After the service, the British man was eager to introduce himself.

"I'm Trevor Martin. This is my wife, Shirley."

"I'm Charles Graham," I replied.

Trevor continued to explain that they were from England and it was their first visit to the United States. Since they had only traveled from their hotel to the conference center, they didn't know anything about Tulsa or what there was to see in the city. I asked them if I could pick them up from their hotel the next morning and treat them to breakfast. They accepted my invitation, and I took them to the Village Inn restaurant near Drysdales, where I was employed. As we ate breakfast, I remember Shirley being uncomfortable because there were men who had not removed their hats before eating. To Shirley, wearing hats while eating was not proper manners and it came as quite a shock.

"They are cowboys and not real formal, as you can see. Tulsa is a cowboy town and that's how they do things here," I explained to Shirley.

That introduction to Oklahoma culture led to my asking Trevor and Shirley if they would like to go next door to Drysdales Western Wear store and get a real feel

175

for Oklahoma. They seemed very excited about going to check out the local flare in clothing.

When we browsed through the store, I placed a Stetson cowboy hat on Trevor -- like the ones he had seen in the movies. He was very pleased by the way he looked in the mirror. Then, I dressed Shirley in a suede jacket with fringe hanging off its arms. Shirley laughed and admired herself in the mirror. Dressing like an authentic American cowboy and cowgirl really loosened them up and they enjoyed the memorable experience.

When I took them back to their hotel, Trevor boldly asked, "Charles, would you be open to coming to England to minister?"

I immediately replied, "I would be honored."

To put things in perspective, this was the summer of 1984, long before cell phones or email. It was the days when we used a pen, some paper, and a stamped envelope to communicate long distance. I received a letter from Trevor asking if I had the month of October available to come to England and minister. I remember clearly that I was in Bruce, Mississippi, when I put together a packet of information and promotional materials to send to him. In the packet, I included a letter that informed him I was available to minister the month of October, and that I would call to give him my flight details.

A week before traveling to England, I made my flight arrangements. I was so green back in those days that it never occurred to me the drastic time difference between Oklahoma, USA and London, England. I simply picked up the phone and called Trevor and Shirley's home. A sleepy voice answered the phone at 4:00 a.m. their time.

"Hello?"

"Hello, Trevor, this is Charles Graham. How're you?"

"Yes. We're fine. And how are you?" Trevor replied in a drowsy tone.

"I'm fine. I'm calling to let you know I'll be arriving at Heathrow tomorrow. I can't wait to see you," I told him excitedly.

On Tuesday, Trevor drove an hour from his home to Heathrow to pick me up. I hadn't arrived yet because I hadn't accounted for the drastic time difference. Trevor was a day early because I had misinformed him.

On Wednesday, I was on the phone in the airport calling Trevor to let him know I had arrived. An hour or so later, Trevor picked me up at the airport. On the way back to Surrey, he stopped at a pub for a bite to eat. I remember feeling uncomfortable when I heard the gentle English pastor order an alcoholic beverage. I wasn't used to seeing ministers drink. I studied the menu and ordered an apple cider, believing I was ordering a non-alcoholic drink. That's when I learned that cider in England is not like the apple cider we consume in the U.S. I discovered that I had ordered an alcoholic drink as well. There I was, personally challenged by his ordering an alcoholic drink, and I did the same thing!

Trevor and I made it to Surrey where Shirley had a meal waiting for us on her dining room table. After several minutes of small-talk, Trevor finally got around to telling me that they hadn't planned for my being there. Trevor admitted that he thought I had been rather presumptuous to simply call and tell him that I was on my way. I was shocked and embarrassed to hear that they never received the information packet I had mailed. I had replied to their invitation, but they had never received the envelope. They had no clue I was coming to England until they got the 4:00 a.m. phone call.

The reality of the news began to wash over me. If they had no clue I was coming, that meant that no ministry was planned, and I had come across the Atlantic Ocean for nothing. My intention was for me to be scheduled to minister the entire month of October in various churches. But in reality, I had arrived in England and I wasn't booked for even one concert. Trevor was right. I did presume. I assumed I would be booked every night during the month. In my mind, I even thought there might be a possibility to meet the Queen.

Embarrassed, I assured Trevor and Shirley that showing up unannounced to minister anywhere was not my style. We both knew that God had not brought me this far for just a vacation. We looked at the calendar and we began to pray God would show us His purpose for my visit.

Trevor's church, The Kings Church, Epson, was a given, but the rest of the month had to be filled in. Trevor stepped into his office, picked up his phone, and began making calls to fellow pastors in the United Kingdom. Trevor was determined to make the best of the situation. I had to smile when he was speaking to one of his minister friends in Scotland.

"Yes, he is a very tall American. Large singing voice," Trevor said tentatively.

I could hear Trevor describing me every way he could imagine, but avoiding the color of my skin. I grabbed a piece of paper and I quickly scribbled the letters b.l.a.c.k. on it.

"I didn't know if I could say that," Trevor smiled.

That's when I began to refer to myself as being *Tall, dark and handsome*. In some cases I would say *extra dark*.

By the time Trevor was finished calling his long list of prospects, there were only five or six days out of that month that I didn't have a concert scheduled. We never understood why the ministry information packet did not arrive. Better yet – what I thought would be a one-time trip to the UK turned into a life-long ministry, and I have been back every year since that memorable October.

To continue the story of my first trip, it probably could go without mentioning, but there weren't arrangements made for a place for me to stay since no one knew I was coming. So, Trevor kindly asked Jean, his secretary, if she would ask her husband about the possibility of my staying with them. Now, Jean is one of the sweetest persons I've ever known. Derek, on the other hand, was not so warm to the idea of the strange American imposing upon them so unexpectedly. In fact, when Jean asked Derek if it were a possibility, his remark was a curt, "Not likely."

Jean began to pray specifically that God would change Derek's heart and he would allow me to stay with them. Later, Derek did have a change of heart. He went to Jean and said:

"If the man is all right with Trevor, he is all right with me."

Years later, Derek admitted that it is now hard to imagine me not being a part of their lives.

Derek and Jean's profession was coach drivers, so when it came to getting me from one place to the next, I was in good hands. They owned a couple of buses and had built a successful transportation business. During that first month in England, Derek acted as my personal driver, taking me everywhere I needed to go. For many years he has met me at the airport when I arrive for ministry. He has also performed the duty of driving me to all my appointments and events.

Derek was one of the finest drivers I had ever seen. He could reverse and park perfectly in seconds, regardless of how narrow the parking space. Also, Derek was never late. When the M25 motorway was backed up to a standstill, he would find the necessary side roads and get me to the airport on time. One day, while trying to catch a departing plane for the United States, I had to inform Derek that I had left my very important briefcase back at his house. Derek drove an hour back to his home, grabbed my briefcase, and made it back in time to hand it to me before my airplane departed.

During that month, I met Pastor Tom Thompson from Hatherleigh. To get to his church, I had to travel by train from Epsom to Exeter, England. At the train station, Reverend Thompson picked me up and we traveled together back to his little village. Along the way, Pastor Tom wanted to visit Christine Bruce, one of his parishioners who was in a hospital in Oakhampton. Because Christine was about to give birth, I felt the last thing she would want to see walking into her hospital room would be a 6'3" black American she had never met.

Reverend Thompson insisted, and before long I was standing in the hospital room with Christine, her husband Ian, and his parents, as I waited my turn to hold the newborn baby. I was last in line as infant David Bruce was passed into my arms. Through the years of my ministry in England, David has found his faith in Jesus, married his lovely wife Hilary, built his family home, and started his family. I had the privilege of witnessing his life develop beautifully, and when I held his first born baby in my arms I began a new journey with the next generation.

People often ask me what I consider to be the most memorable part of my travels around the world. From the French Riviera, to the fjords of Norway, to the rolling hills of Scotland, and to the lakes of England, it is always the people in all those places who make the miles worth traveling.

I have always had a heart for people. But, as in America, not all people in England are comfortable about being around a minister. Often I would see a wife and her children attending church together. Many times, the father of the family chose not to attend a service, or perhaps he was not even a Christian. There were several occasions when I would find myself visiting in homes and the husbands would make themselves scarce.

I prayed that God would help me relate to the aloof fathers and husbands. If I was staying with a family and the man of the house disappeared for work early in the morning, I would deliberately make my way to the fields, find him, and develop a friendship with the husband as he was milking, mucking, or plowing.

One of the gentlemen I encountered was named Malcom. He was a potter. When I heard him working one morning, I made my way out to his pottery shed. He was aloof at first, but when I made the effort to connect with him, a great friendship and brotherhood was forged. As a result of that kind of effort, I witnessed salvations, baptisms, and ministry in the lives of some of several men.

On one early morning, I met with a brother in the barn who had experienced a moral failure in his life. I asked God for wisdom, and I knew the first step was to care for him and extend God's love to him. When I reached the barn that morning, there wasn't room in his heart for any conversation. He was suffering. But, through persistence and love, we found mutual grounds for a healing conversation. After some time, I watched God restore him to his wife, to his family, and to his ministry.

I traveled to Scotland where I was connected to a wonderful couple from The Kings Church of Motherwell. Reverend Hugh Clark was serving as pastor with his wife, Sheila. As I ministered at the church, I was housed for the week with members, Eddie and Hannah Jeffery. When I arrived at their home I was immediately immersed into Scotland's language and culture.

Motherwell is a working class industry town filled with tall apartment towers and down-to-earth people. I'll never forget when I was introduced to Hannah and Eddie, and then left alone to converse with them. Even though we were all speaking some form of English, our accents prevented us from fully understanding each other. We found ourselves laughing hysterically at our situation.

"Would you like a cup of tea?" was all they were asking of me, but it took an excruciating amount of my brainpower to understand.

The first night I was in Scotland, I called back to the U.S. to speak to my sister and brother-in-law. I thought it would be fun to ask my brother-in-law, John, to attempt to speak with Eddie.

"All I could make out was poor Eddie saying *Pardon? Pardon?* I was on the floor and I couldn't stop laughing.

In poor Eddie's defense, it took some time for my new friends and me to understand each other. Thank goodness they had a terrific sense of humor. It's a good thing, because most of my memory is of our laughing together.

On a side note: I remember making the observation that whoever the persons are who build doors in Scotland, they must be some of the richest folks in the country. Not only does every room have a door, but every hallway has doors as well. If you walk into the hallway, you have to open a door. If you wish to enter the kitchen, you have to go through the kitchen door. Because of coldness in Scotland, installing doors helps to heat their homes more efficiently.

Eddie was a very talented young man. When he was young, Eddie was invited to New York City to sing in an evangelistic crusade. He possessed a great tenor voice and on several occasions I was blessed to sing with him at his church in Motherwell. His church had a love for God and an amazing amount of love for me.

While I was ministering in Scotland, I also performed open-air concerts. During one of those concerts, a man who had been drinking too much attempted to converse with me as I was singing.

"You're a big one, aren't ya, bub?"

He had no ill intention, but he just wanted to visit with me.

"Hey!" he repeated, "I said you're a big one, aren't ya, bub?

I just smiled and kept singing.

At that time, unemployment in that region of Scotland was very high. Despite the lack of funds, the Lord called the congregation to build a new church. It was an honor and blessing for me to be with them on their groundbreaking day. We gathered at the site where they used to have church and we walked together to the new location. The event was newsworthy and a local TV news reporter posed the question on many minds of the citizens: *How do you intend to pay for this new church during our economic downturn?* I'll never forget Pastor Clark looking at the skeptical reporter and saying:

"Without sounding presumptuous, God will pay for it."

The reporter had no response after the pastor gave the responsibility back to the Lord.

I traveled one day to sing at a school in Scotland, and I got another glimpse of the negative impact of prejudice and hatred in a community. Because of the country's history, something as simple as the color green sparked hostility and hatred. The bitterness and separation got so bad that the authorities had to install a wire mesh over the green light in the traffic signal because the color green represented an opposing view to some.

It got so bad that when a Subway restaurant franchise moved into the community, they were informed that they couldn't use green in their famous green and yellow logo. It is a tangible way to show just how deep hatred runs when certain colors on the spectrum trigger hate towards another human being. I spoke candidly to the young people and told them that the solution to hatred in America wasn't brought about by legislation but by the love of Jesus. The same must be true in Scotland, I reminded them. I shared with them that I grew up in a community where I experienced discrimination firsthand and I had a choice to make. I could either carry the hurt in my life, or I could work to develop past it.

"Here in this community, someone hasn't grown past it. I grew not because the conditions changed, but because I changed," I said to them.

It's wonderful how certain songs become a part of your life journey. Songs that stick in my mind as I reminisce about the UK are the songs I would sing with the children. I would invite them up on the stage to sing songs such as, *He's Still Working on Me* and *I Am a Promise*. They were the most requested songs when I visited England and when I hear them now, they bring back sweet memories.

One of my more humorous experiences in Motherwell was the day a young man in the church wanted to show me around his place of employment. He worked in one of the United Kingdom's most prestigious suit factories, Daxs Simpson.

We fit everyone is the proud byline they use in their advertising, so I looked forward to their fitting me in a suit that looked just like the one they had recently fitted for The Prince of Wales. What seemed like a simple task for one of the greatest suit companies in world, turned into awkward moment to say the least. After trying to fit me in one of their finest suits, they may have considered changing their motto to: *We fit everyone but Charles Graham*.

After several valiant attempts, the manager who could provide perfect apparel for the president of the United States and the Prince of Wales could not fit me!

When you are in Scotland, many things are referred to as being "wee." Well, in my case, I suppose I just wasn't wee enough to fit in a Daxs suit. Everyone but the manager got a good laugh from the awkward situation.

Speaking of Scottish apparel, Reverend Clark's daughter Karen was scheduled to get married and it was at her wedding where I wore my first Scottish kilt. My friends, Terrance and Betty, took me to Glasgow to a kilt hire (rental) shop. The shop assistant was shocked to discover the person looking for a kilt was not the Scottish man with me, but rather the 6'3" black American standing in front of him.

Because I was going to get my photo taken at a nearby photography studio, he offered to wave the rental fee if I would allow him to properly dress me, and then I would agree to walk several blocks down Buchanan Street to the studio. I reluctantly accepted his offer. He took the kilt off the hanger and told me how to attire myself with each piece of the outfit.

For several minutes, I put on what I knew how to put on, but when I walked out of the dressing room holding several leftover pieces of the outfit in each hand —a sporran (a leather pouch) in one hand and a sgian dubh (a knife) in the other—I agreed it was necessary for him to step in and help. He laughed and began to dress me properly in each piece of the full Scottish kilt. The thing that looked like a fanny pack wasn't worn behind me, but in front of me. The assistant laughed as he positioned each item in its proper place.

Fully dressed, I walked courageously down one of Glasgow's busiest shopping districts as agreed. People passed by and I often heard remarks such as, *It suits ya.* I learned later that my photograph hung in the photo studio window for a few weeks after the shoot.

At the reception, I was announced as Charles Graham of the Clan Montrose. The name Graham is of Scottish origin. I was announced and the cameras flashed as I appeared in my full-dress kilt.

My closest friends may tell you that it doesn't bother me at all to be a "fish out of water." When you look at people in an equal way, you find yourself treating everyone with the same respect. I enjoy being the man from Southern California while traveling through the UK.

I have had the privilege of visiting elementary and secondary schools in the UK and I have always found joy in communicating with young people. When I opened up my time for questions and answers, inevitably I would be asked if I knew Mickey Mouse. They figured anyone who lives in California must know the most famous Disney "person" from Southern California. They also asked what kind of car I drove. In the beginning of my ministry there I proudly told the kids that I drove a van. They immediately envisioned the black and grey van with the red stripe from the hit American television show, "The A Team."

"You drive a van like B.A.'s?" they asked excitedly.

No, my van wasn't customized like the A team's van. I'm sure they were hoping my poor old maroon van had a bold red stripe and big red wing spoiler.

The students would also ask me about American sports, specifically baseball. As you have learned from earlier chapters, I was the guy who was most comfortable making posters for a sporting event, not the guy on the court or on the field playing the game. One day, a couple of boys named Peter and James, asked me if I would teach them some things about baseball.

"I'll go in the backyard and teach you what I know," I offered.

The guys were excited to get some input from a real American about our great American pastime. Admittedly, after a few minutes, the guys were graciously teaching me how to play baseball.

Beyond my awkward start in ministry in the UK, God opened the doors of ministry to annual journeys. I attended minister conferences and various pastors connected me with their friends and fellow churches. The churches included the Church of England, Church of Scotland, Church of Wales, the Methodists, the Congregationalists, the Baptists, and independent fellowships.

The spiritual climate in the UK is much like it is here in the United States. There is a hunger and searching for a bigger purpose in life, not just church attendance. When I started my ministry there, most traditional churches were losing members, but the stirring among people and the House Church Movement was beginning to develop. People were finding alternative ways and places to worship, and churches outside the parameters and definition of the established churches were flourishing. That had an impact on my ministry as well. I found myself receiving invitations to sing and teach in nontraditional church settings with people who were seeking a spiritual experience. To say the least, it was an exciting time for church growth and a blessed time to be a part of the change.

When I arrived to my first conference in the UK, the sole purpose of gathering was to pray together and to support one another in order to form a powerful spiritual brotherhood. It was a fresh start to me because by the time I arrived in Great Britain I had begun to see in the United States some unfortunate levels of preference being given to big ministries versus the small. In the United Kingdom there was no preferential treatment of the ministers of large congregations over the smaller ones. Sadly, over the years, the UK followed the same trend, and I began to notice less leading by God, and more human order coming into play, still church growth spread across the country.

One church in which I ministered was a former movie cinema that seated eighteen hundred. The venue was packed with people from around the world and the main speaker was German born, Reverend Reinhard Bonnke. His ministry was in the continent of Africa. As I looked around the room at the notable men and women of God, I was reminded of the words that the Lord had impressed upon me as my ministry grew: *The bigger I am in you, the smaller the world will be to you.*

Effective ministry through this period happened in converted cinemas, theaters, town halls, schools and homes. It was evident that God was blessing the hunger and desire in those who were seeking Him. Whether I was preaching, singing, conducting workshops, ministering in outreaches, or performing in public schools, I consistently found new places to minister during this time.

As I traveled in other countries I discovered that the Holy Spirit is the same. Also, basic human need is the same. Accents, language, and culture may have been different, but two basic things remain the same: man's need of God, and God's love of man.

AFRICA

My first invitation to Africa came as I was
attending a conference for ministers held in England. I
met minister named Gary Strong, and he invited me to
Harare, Zimbabwe where he served as pastor at the Kings
Church. Pastor Strong had made it known that he was
excited for me to come to his church. Although he was
white, I assumed that Pastor Strong's church
congregation in Africa was black. To my surprise, his
church congregation was mainly white.

The ministry at the church was also connected to
a crusade that featured Reinhard Bonnke. That's when I
learned that Reverend Bonnke had been reaching the lost
in Africa since 1967. His ministry was effective and
popular on the continent. It was the first time I had ever
seen a tent with 40,000 people under it!

The gathering was called the "Fire Conference"
and I was invited to sing. I remember the conference
lasted a week out in a field, and I also remember that the
assembly received strong opposition from the Muslim
community. Despite the opposition, during one of the
services thousands of Christians prayed for an eight-year-
old Muslim girl who could not hear. The child was
instantly and dramatically healed.

"How do you feel about God healing your
daughter?" Reverend Bonnke asked her father.

The Muslim father replied, "I will love and trust
the God who brought healing to my daughter."

Just like during Jesus's ministry of healing the
sick, the miraculous healing of the eight-year-old spread

through the community. Witnessing that miracle was a faith-building experience for me.

The night before flying out of Harare, I was invited to minister at a youth meeting. I spoke to the young people gathered there and encouraged them in their walk with the Lord. We prayed together, and after the meeting I noticed a skeptical young man lingering and not leaving with the other youth.

He and I sat on the front porch of my friend's home and we began a conversation that went on for hours. We talked through the entire night until the sun began to rise the next morning. I continually assured him that God knew him better than I knew him, and I let him know that it wasn't my job to get him saved but to share with him the truth of God's love.

"God knows who you are. Whatever questions you have, God has the answers," I told him with conviction.

The young man wasn't ready to commit to God, so we left things where they were.

"As a Christian I would like to say, 'goodbye, my brother,' but for now, I will say, 'goodbye, my friend,'" I told him as I left.

About three months later, I received a letter from him. I anxiously opened it because I needed to know where he was spiritually.

"Hello, my brother in Christ!" the letter began.

The words in his letter were a real moment of growth for me in my walk with the Lord. It was like the words in the Bible when Paul said he had planted, Apollos had watered, but God had given the increase. It was the point in my life when I learned to release another person's journey.

While teaching at Roffey Place Bible College in Horsham, West Suffix, England, I met two students named, David and Ruth Ndaruhutse. I had met David and his wife Ruth while on a ministry trip. They had been studying in a Bible school in England. After a morning session, David walked up to me.

"You're coming to Burundi, Africa," David said with confidence.

I didn't think much of it until about a decade later, while living in California. My pastor invited me to a breakfast meeting and to my surprise the gentleman sitting across from me looked very familiar.

"Hello, Charles," he began. "You probably don't remember me, but I met you in England about ten years ago. I'm the man who told you that you would go to Burundi, Africa."

Of course, I remembered David. I had heard inspirational stories about his walking through Africa. They were amazing stories such as; David would receive a word from God and then travel any distance to share the gospel of Jesus. He did as he was told and people's lives were changed for eternity because of his obedience. His relationship with the Lord was so extraordinary that I was truly humbled to be in his presence.

After knowing David for several years, I traveled to his beautiful home country of Burundi. But, as God would have it, prior to my visit, David died in a tragic plane crash. It was a deep blow to me because I had a strong desire to fellowship more with the incredible servant of God.

I was told that when the first responders made it to the site of the airplane crash, they found David lying with his arms folded across his chest as if he died peacefully. That bittersweet news didn't surprise me. God took that devoted servant to Heaven in peace.

I also learned that during his last crusade, David placed his coat on his nephew, indicating that there would be a change in the ministry. In his spirit, David knew it was time to pass along the mantle of leadership to the next generation. After that meeting, David boarded the plane that crashed.

My journey to Burundi actually started with a layover for a few hours in Nairobi. I flew from London, England and met Pastor Peter Sila and his wife, Dorothy from the Living Word church in Nairobi. Their son, Solomon, picked me up at the airport and I thought it was unusual that he asked if I wanted to pray before he drove back to their home.

"That's okay, Solomon. You can pray," I told him.

Solomon prayed and we left the airport. As soon as he drove down the first street, I fully realized why he felt the need to pray. The traffic was the wildest traffic I had ever experienced in my life. There was no such thing as traffic patterns or organized driving. Yes, there were two lanes, but drivers could go any direction at any time they wanted using those two lanes. I had never experienced such traffic chaos. I'm sure my jaw was dropped and my mouth was wide open as Solomon drove me through the streets of Nairobi.

The Sila's graciously hosted me for about twelve hours before my flight to Burundi departed. While in their home, they invited me to come back in the future to minister in Kenya. It took some time, but I eventually accepted their invitation.

After my time with the Sila family, it was time to return to the airport. Before Solomon put the car into gear, I volunteered to pray a prayer of protection over us. One trip on those streets helped me fully understand why a prayer before traveling was important. You'll never appreciate the gravity of the miracle if you never take the journey. My ministry time in Burundi started with David Ndaruhutse's nephew, Pastor Edmond Kivuye, the pastor of Eglise Vivante in Burundi, and the director of African Revival Ministries. When I arrived at the airport, Pastor Edmond met me in the terminal.

My first trip to Harare, Zimbabwe, Africa had been life-changing. Being immersed in the culture stretched me in ways that I hadn't expected. But, my second trip that took me to Burundi was much more impactful. I always said that I was raised in a poor home in a poor southern Arkansas town, but when I saw the immense poverty and need in Burundi, I realized what real poverty looked like. Burundi, I learned, was a very significant country in Africa that the Lord had waiting for me.

When I arrived in Burundi, I was overwhelmed by the need. Poverty's face and reality greeted me at the airport and what money I had in my wallet and pockets I handed out in the first few minutes of being there. The desperately poor people and the eyes of those deprived little boys and girls reaching out to me, was more than I could bear.

"Lord, I pray ... show me where I can make a difference," was all I could pray through my tears.

When you are broken-hearted and you cry out to God, it's amazing how sometimes his reply will ring out with unparalleled clarity.

"I didn't bring you to Africa for you to cure all the ills of this country. I brought you here because I have assignments for you," The Lord said to me.

I approached the vastness of the needs in Africa by going back to God and letting him lead me. I have done that now for twenty plus years. I drew my inspiration from the actions of Jesus, remembering how he walked through the mass of people on a daily basis during his brief public ministry. He would touch and heal those that the Father led Him to.

It reminds me of my position I hold today with the adoption advocacy charity, Adopt This Child. There is no greater calling than to help an orphan find security and a home. The need across our world is unending and vast, but we cannot be overwhelmed by its magnitude. We must go forward leaning on the provision of the Lord based upon His direction.

Pastor Edmond and his wife, Faith, graciously welcomed me into their world. They took me to their home where they introduced me to local African cuisine. Although the food had different names, it was similar to what I had eaten during my childhood. For instance, my mother would prepare collard or turnip greens from the garden. In Burundi, African greens were smashed, ground and cooked to a spinach consistency. They called it isombe.

The ministry schedule began with morning prayer at 5:00 a.m. A few hours later we held a morning ministry meeting. That led us to the noon ministry meeting. A few minutes after the noon ministry time we had an afternoon prayer time. Of course, we held an evening ministry meeting as well. At that time in my life, I was fresh out of Bible school and I was not expecting to preach five services a day. After the first two days I felt as though I had preached everything I had learned in Bible school! I was under the assumption that I would be required to preach one sermon a day, not five, but I simply leaned on God to help me and I truly felt like God was ministering to me. He was so faithful to give me the right words to minister.

Preaching and teaching were not my only ministries. I also served in a childrens home that was designed give kids a place to live until they could move out. It was much like a foster home in the United States. A friend from England named, Chrissie Chapman, ran the home. Chrissie was a midwife, and then became director of a ministry called C.R.I.B., which stands for "children rescued in Burundi."

African Revival Ministries consisted of Eglise Vivante church, a hospital, several medical clinics, C.R.I.B. childrens home, schools and feeding programs throughout Burundi. I saw firsthand the value of all the ministries they had developed under the guidance of the Lord. Through Pastor Edmond, I met lead surgeon Dr. Euloge and his wife, medical director and surgeon, Dr. Aline Muryango who also worked for African Revival Ministries. Dr. Euloge served as my translator. The needs in Burundi were great and at times often overwhelming to the medical and ministry personnel. I had never seen a more dedicated group of doctors working so sacrificially on a daily basis. It inspired me.

I wish I could do justice in words to describe adequately the exuberance and energy in a Burundian church service. To say that music is important to their worship is a gross understatement. The praise and worship portion of the service might last for two hours.

Keep in mind that many Burundians have to travel several hours from their village to attend the church. Once they were in the House of the Lord, they didn't seem in any rush to leave.

Also in church, my attention was drawn to all the crippled and lame. Everyone was welcome into the fellowship, despite who they were, what they were going through, or even what tribal differences they had. Of the two thousand people in attendance, every family had been affected in some way by the Rwandan genocide. They either lost family members, or lost friends in the horrible violence. It was incredible to witness people who were once mortal enemies standing in the same room and becoming one in the Spirit of God.

The burden I had for the Africans was heavy. I cried many nights as I asked God for wisdom to do what I was asked to do, and do it in the right way. One of the most profound things that happened in my heart may seem strange to some, but it was necessary. I had a simple request of my new African friends. I encouraged the African people to look at me when I spoke to them. It was their nature to look down as I talked to them, but I wanted their eyes to meet mine in order to validate their humanity. That connection was very important to me. Even if I had nothing physically to offer them, I could offer them the love that comes from Christ, and I could acknowledge in that subtle but profound way that they were human beings with value.

One Sunday morning, before arriving at the church, we were informed that there had been a massacre at a refugee camp just outside the city. Pastors, doctors and volunteers assembled and we made our way to a refugee camp. Although I had no idea what we were about to witness, it was not the kind of situation one can understand until actually seeing it for oneself.

The team of rescuers arrived to the "tent city" refugee camp to find only a few tents still standing. Scattered through the camp we saw the charred and burning bodies of dozens of adult victims. Around the camp were thirty-eight little children crying, or simply sitting in shock. Some children were clutching the lifeless bodies of their parents.

I stood back as the medical personnel searched desperately for survivors. They hurriedly picked up babies in their arms and carried them from the horrific scene. I lifted my camera to take pictures of the massacre, but what I saw through my viewfinder became too overwhelming for me to take in.

After doing all we could do, we rushed the children back to the hospital where they were cared for and protected. Later, we attended the worship service as scheduled and the pastor addressed the congregation to inform them as to what had happened. Prayers were offered and the congregation prayed for the victims, their families, and the orphan babies we had rescued from the unbelievable scene.

It's safe to say I cried every day for the next two weeks as the images and the reality of the massacre lingered in my memory. As I write this book many years away from that day of horror, I still can't bring myself to develop the roll of film that captured the moment that changed my life. The massacre in the refugee camp marked the beginning of the New Hope Orphanage in Burundi, as well as my relationship with that ministry.

In America, we tend to paint Africa with a broad brush. We think of exotic wild animals, vast deserts, and intriguing tribal people, but one of my takeaways after ministering in the vast continent for three decades is that the country is as diverse as the needs one finds there.

We must allow our faith to have a voice. I was being driven through the city of Bujumbura one day, and I had just shared the story about how my siblings and I had built a new house for my mother.

My brothers and sisters were full of joy and bursting with pride when we helped our sweet mother transition from the old house, to a brand new home complete with all the modern conveniences. After sharing the story of Mother's new home, a young man in Africa, named Raphael, wanted to show me the home he had proudly built for his dear mother. We drove by his home and he pointed to a lean-to structure with a corrugated tin roof. The simple little structure was the house he had constructed for his mother. The story in my sermon about building Mother's new house had prompted Raphael to do the same for his mother. The value and importance of God's words impressed even deeper upon me at that humble moment.

It's not my word making the difference, but God's words coming through me.

Before I left Burundi, it was my desire to anoint with oil the babies in the childrens home. Children who could have been left alone, with no one to care for them, had been brought into the home where they received food, daily care, and most of all, love from Chrissie.

I remember the first time I walked into the room where the babies were and my first reaction was a broken heart. Tears came to my eyes as I saw the little ones in their cribs. Some of the babies were crawling and some were sitting on the floor. Disappointment came over me when I tried to get close to any of them. They would recoil and cry in fear. The sweet babies were used to Chrissie's touch and her white skin. When I came in the room, they were frightened because I was a stranger to them.

I was disappointed when I left the babies that day. But, I was resolved to try to connect with them the next day. Unfortunately, one day turned into two and each day after, the results were the same—they would cry and I would leave dejected. All I wanted was to hold the babies, pray for them, and anoint them with oil.

My ministry trip in Burundi was coming to an end and my bags were packed when I went back to the childrens home for one last visit. As I looked into the eyes of the babies in the cribs, and the few precious ones crawling on the floor, suddenly, one of the babies broke rank and crawled toward me!

Little Gideon made his way to me and without protest he allowed me to pick him up. He smiled at me as I held him in my arms. You can imagine the thrill in my heart as I began to cry tears of joy. It was as if Gideon was the leader of the group. All the other babies grew silent and watched curiously. One by one, Gideon's little friends allowed me to anoint them and pray for them before I had to leave.

That little leader of the babies is now a teenager. Over the years, I have watched the children grow and I have met many more who have grown up in the childrens home and orphanage. The first group of babies have developed into young adults, pursued careers, and become parents. Many of the African children left the country to attend colleges and universities in the UK and in the US.

I've been blessed to host the students who have been able to come to the United States. Recently, I watched several of our students walk across the stage at Oklahoma Christian University to receive their diplomas. Some have even received master's degrees in fields of engineering, business, communications and medicine. Because I have an intimate knowledge of their difficult and humble beginnings in Africa, it is even more special for me as I watch God's blessings in their lives. What a tremendous reward for me to see some of the students who were rescued from the burning village, and saved from literal ashes of despair, now live lives that display the unfailing goodness of the Lord.

Among the first group of orphans there was a baby named Grace. I have watched Grace grow from a fearful little girl into a young lady finding balance in faith and God. She earned her communications degree at Oklahoma Christian University. It makes me feel good to know that the students are living out the scripture, Jeremiah 29:11— *For I know the plans that I have for you, says the LORD, plans for peace and not for evil, to give you a future and a hope.*

Being in Africa opened my eyes and helped me live my Christian life more boldly. I have learned to be thankful for the little things that I used to take for granted. For instance, the first year I would fight ants that would crawl towards my food. The next year, I learned to brush away the ants, and by the third year when they fell in my tea, I considered ants to be extra protein.

Traveling the world to minister God's love has truly changed my life. As I wrote this chapter regarding my ministry in different countries, I was sitting in Paddington Station in London, England. The hustle and bustle of the citizens of London as well as tourists from around the world reminded me of just how far I had come on my wonderful journey. Trains moving in and out of Paddington Station provided a symbol for me as I considered how my dreams have continually evolved and shifted from one track to another, and yet, my destination has remained the same.

Since the moment I handed my life over to the leading of the Holy Spirit, I have been a passenger on a spiritual train. Some days my destination has been pre-planned and ordered, just like the workings of a train schedule. My ticket was clearly marked and punched and I had a very clear vision of where God wanted me to be.

The spontaneous parts of my journey have me moving randomly through moments and even seconds of connections. I call those moments, "divine appointments" because there really is no other way to define it when you are a child of the King. I could fill another hundred pages of this book telling you of all the appointments in my journey that have His divine stamp upon them.

Sitting on that bench in Paddington, I allowed myself a moment to breathe, look around me and let it all soak in. I took time to reflect on the shear physical distance I had traveled from Boydell, Baxter and Dermott, Arkansas to many parts of God's creation. My physical body (that same body that begrudgingly dragged a sack across the cotton fields of Arkansas as I yearned to escape) has literally moved through country after country, covering thousands of miles. I have been blessed to minister over the many years on multiple continents that now embrace me as one of their own. I surrendered my will to His will and because I pursued vigorously what God wanted for my life, He took me where He wanted me to be. How thankful I am to have been given this wonderful privilege. I don't let a day go by without telling the Lord how grateful I am for his constant presence and direction for my days.

Thank You, Lord, for these international doors of ministry you opened, and the ministers who graciously allowed me to walk along with them over the past 35 years:

Ministries in the United Kingdom

Pastors Geri & Michelle De Somma
Carmel City Church
Bristol, England

Rev. Ian McFarlane and Rev. Steve Elemes
Bookham Baptist Church
Bookham, England

Derek & Jean Jones and Jenny Jones
Assisted in ministry at
Bookham, England

Pastors Jonathan & Karen Dunning
Meadowhead Christian Fellowship
Sheffield, England

Pastors Jim & Cynthia Wilkerson
Hollybush Christian Fellowship
Thirsk, England

Rev. Tom & Rosemary Thompson
The Vine Christian Fellowship
Hatherleigh, England

Oz and Olive Squier
Ian and Christine Bruce
Herbert and Sadie Bruce
Assisted in ministry
Hatherleigh, England

Rev. Allister & Myra Lewis
Cullumpton Fellowship
Cullumpton, England

Rev. Bob and Hilda Gordon
Ministers John & Angie Hindmarsh
Kingdom Faith Ministries
Norwich, England

Rev. Trevor & Shirley Martin
The Kings Fellowship
Epsom, England

Rev. Derek & Maureen Brown
Minister Peter & Ema Brown
The Kings Church
Aldershot, England

Rev. Dennis & Helene Greenidge
Worldwide Mission Fellowship
West Norwood, London, England

Rev. Graham & Maureen Poland
Grosvenor Church
Barnstaple, England

Mervyn & June Mitchell
Assisted in ministry a
Barnstaple, England

Malcolm & Jean Hutchinson
Assisted in ministry at
Kirkby Stephen, England

Pastors Lewis & Ruth Staley
Barnard Castle Christian Fellowship
Bernard Castle, England

Pastors Stephen & Sarah Brindley
Crossways Community Church
Stone Kent, England

Pastors Robbie & Donna Howells
Newport City Church
Newport, Wales

Mr. & Mrs. Richard Shepard
Mr. & Mrs. Graham Shepard
Mr. & Mrs. Martin Shepard
The Warehouse Cathedral
Newport, Wales

Roger & Brenda Jones
Assisted in ministry at
Painscastle, Wales

Pastors Peter & Sherrie Hadden
Rhema Christian Centre Ministries
Kirkcaldy, Scotland

Pastors Bernie & Nan McLaughlin
The Bridge Church
Kilwinning, Scotland

Pastors Joe & Yvonne Ewing
Riverside Church
Banff, Scotland

Pastors George & Mary Alexander
Dunfermline Christian Centre
Dunfermline, Scotland

Rev. Hugh & Shelia Clark
Paul & Heather Foinette
David & Barbara Ramage
The Kings Church
Motherwell, Scotland

James & Rhoda Reid
David & Jeanette Swann
Terrence & Betty McBurney
Assisted in ministry at
Motherwell, Scotland

Ministries in Africa

Pastor Edmond & Faith Kivuye
Dr. Euloge & Dr. Aline Muryango
Pastor Ruben Kinyama
African Revival Ministries, Eglise Vivante Church
Bujumbura, Burundi

Pastors Straton & Adeliene Gataha
African Revival Ministries, Eglise Vivante Church
Kigali, Rwanda

Pastors Titus & Purity Kiange
Living Word Church
Kyumbi, Kenya

Pastors Peter & Dorthy Sila
Solomon & Carlene Nashilu Saropa Sila
Micah & Zipporah Sila
Living Word Church
Nairobi, Kenya

Pastors Donald & Tabitha Mutiso,
Living Word Church
Nairobi, Kenya

CHAPTER 16

"Recordings"

My love for music blossomed when I began my college career in Missouri. As I mentioned in a previous chapter, I participated in my college talent show and for the first time, I was singing in front of a large audience. When I finished singing I received a surprising round of applause. My heart was full of excitement as I dreamed of performing more in the future.

In 1976, the Southwest Baptist College Baptist Student Union sponsored me in a concert for the student body, and my dream took a leap forward. Composer and pianist, Jerry Estes, agreed to accompany me that evening during the concert. The reaction from the audience that night was more confirmation that God had something prepared for me.

To my surprise, a student shared with me a recording he made of my concert that night. He had a simple cassette recorder that he held in his hand over the rail of the second level seating area. You can only imagine the third-rate recording quality of such a set up. Nonetheless, I was anxious to hear the recording because the crowd that night had even called for an encore. I thought to myself, *God must have tweaked the listening ears of my audience to make me sound much better than I really did.* I knew that God had blinded eyes in the past, so he certainly had the power to deafen some ears. My performance was not very good. In fact, some of my relatives who have heard the cassette still bring it up on occasion and mimic my cracking voice.

After many years of God's grace being poured into my life, I continued to grow and develop my singing ability. I was so thankful to God for every opportunity he had given me and I could not believe I was actually entering a recording studio to make my first recording. In 1981, I went to Smyrna, Georgia to record in the Twelve Oaks Studio. My friend, Reid Hall, had begun his engineering career and he was the perfect guy to take me, a raw and inexperienced singer, and show me the ropes to making a professional recording.

I entered the recording industry almost completely clueless. What I knew about the experience of making a record was what I had acquired from being a consumer of music. I purchased albums and cassettes and I listened carefully to the singers, instruments, and arrangements. A few concerts I attended gave me some ideas about performance, but nothing about what it took to record the songs on an album. The behind-the-scenes efforts of what it took to make a record was like going to a foreign country and singing in a foreign language.

Because the recording engineer was a friend, Reid and I did a lot of the preliminary preparation in his home. His friendship also meant that I could lean on his knowledge of studio etiquette and techniques, and it also meant that Reid was happy to graciously walk me through the uncharted territory. For instance, I wasn't used to singing full voice in an empty room with no audience present. My singing experiences were mostly being surrounded by people in a worship setting. So, my initial lesson learned was, it is easier to sing to someone than to no one.

Before my time with Reid, I had missed words, and on occasion, rewrote a song or two in mid-stream. In the studio, I didn't have the luxury of singing through a mishap. Reid had developed a terrific ear for hearing missed pronounced words.

My first moment standing in a soundproof recording booth was surreal. There I was, putting on headphones and looking through the soundproof glass at a professional engineer. I was excited but also sobered by the thought of all the work ahead.

I wanted my mother to experience the excitement of my first time in the studio as well. We traveled to Atlanta and we stayed in adjacent hotel rooms. We got up early each morning, had breakfast and spent our days together. Of course, my mother was up very early to make her hotel bed and clean the room as if she were preparing it for the next guest. Old habits are hard to break. She even made friends with the maid who would show up and have nothing to clean or straighten. They would sit on the end of the bed and share stories as they got to know each other.

In the recording studio, Mother would stay in the engineering suite as Reid recorded my singing. Because we were getting up early and going to bed late, she was becoming exhausted. One day, Reid turned on the talk-back microphone so I could hear my sleeping mother snoring behind him. He was a good sport to let Mother stay in there with him and get some rest.

Making a record was not only a momentous time for me, but it meant a lot to my family. It was an opportunity to thank my dad who had taught me so much about hard work and who had instilled his knowledge and wisdom in me. I appreciated my dad's efforts to raise us all in a home where God is loved. I knew he would have been proud of my making an album that honored God and my family.

I was out of town the day my brother called to tell me that the boxes of my new album had arrived on the porch. My whole town seemed to be celebrating the album and he was quick to tell me that many in the community had lined up at our house to buy the first copies.

"How much do we sell them for, Charles?"

"Eight dollars will be fine," I told him.

"I know we can get fifteen dollars. How about fifteen dollars?"

"No. Eight will be fine," I assured him.

He wasn't happy with my decision, but he did as I requested and sold the new records for eight dollars. As for my mother, she was happy to tell all the buyers and townsfolk that she was there when the recording happened. It was a proud day for my whole family.

Besides the looks on my family's faces, my favorite memory of that first recording was the process of creating the best possible album cover. In those days, I was taking my lead from other gospel music performers who were professional, and who had been recording for many years. In vogue on albums were photos of singers standing on bridges, sitting in trees, or standing by fireplaces in a home setting. I chose standing by the fireplace.

I was living in Independence, Missouri, at the time and I would often visit a couple from my church named Bill and Elvita Hanson. I affectionately called them Grandma and Grandpa Hanson. By the time I made the album, Grandpa had passed away, unfortunately. Grandma had a lovely fireplace in her home and one day as she was away at work, I brought in a photographer to capture my image in front of her fireplace. The photographer had a nice studio we could have used, but that fireplace shot was already in my head as I envisioned the cover of the album.

I was managing a clothing store, of course, and brown tweed was the rage. I bought a brown tweed jacket and wore it over a nice open collar shirt. That's what all the really good-looking men on album covers were doing in the early eighties. There I was; standing with my foot up on the hearth and my elbow resting on the mantle. I was thin. I had my hair cut just right and everything in my mind had lined up perfectly.

The photographer set up his gear and he started shooting as if we were in his studio. I was so focused on my look that I didn't take time to notice just how out of place the bay window behind me looked in the composition of the picture. I also didn't notice that the ash on the hearth from a recent fire in the fireplace. To top it off, Grandma's grandson, Jim jokingly told me later that the two blurred photos in the double picture frames on the mantle were pictures of his brother, Bill, and him. I never even noticed the pictures of the two little white boys when I was standing there in my perfect pose. Actually, I didn't notice anything but me.

Making choices for what songs I record on albums is a prayerful process. My desire is to share songs that minister to me, hoping that God will use them to minister to others. Songs I chose for my first album content included, *My Tribute, We Are The Reason, Praise the Lord, Lighthouse, Wherever He Leads I'll Go, Light At The End of Your Darkness* and *Thank You Lord.*

I continued my singing ministry traveling with albums people could purchase. I wanted them to enjoy the music in their homes long after I left their town. I'm happy I have recordings available, but I have always left it to the pastor or host to mention they are obtainable after a concert. The purpose of the recorded music is to serve as an extension of my ministry.

My second album was recorded in the late 1980s. One of my favorite gospel singers at that time was Sandi Patti, the artist who had made the song *We Shall Behold Him* very popular. I wanted to record that song and title the album after it. At that time in my ministry, I was living in Tulsa and I was privileged to record in Castle Church Studios, a company founded by Leon Russell in the 1970s.

I have grown to love the song list on that record. It has classic tunes such as *He is Jehovah, Precious Blood, Blow the Trumpet, Charity, Let Us Rejoice, Star of the Morning, Sacrifice of Praise and We Will Stand.* After the release of this album, *We Shall Behold Him* became my signature song and remains so to this day.

On a lighter note, I remember the album cover when I think of those recording sessions. In the late eighties, I was strongly influenced by singer/songwriter, Lionel Richie; not just his voice and talent but also his hair. A set of twins, Todd and Tyler from Sedalia, Missouri, used to say my hair looked like the cover of a microphone. They were referring to the black pop screens we used to put over the microphones.

I was aware enough by this time to not have my picture taken in a house in front of a fireplace. Instead, I bought a nice suit from Drysdales Western Wear and hired a professional photographer. Unfortunately, when I looked at the album cover, all I could see was my big thumb pointing to the word "Behold" below me. I refer to that album as the one with the thumb. Once you notice it, the thumb is all you see!

I dedicated the record to a friend of mine from Marietta, Georgia, named Steve Leary. Steve was a wonderful brother in the Lord who showed me what Christ-like love looks like. One day, I commented on a new sweater he was wearing and before I knew it, Steve had taken off the sweater and placed it in my bag. I tried to give it back to him but he wanted me to have it. I learned that when one gives something that they consider something of value, that's when true giving happens.

My third album reminds me that we were making records in the LP and cassette days. The title song and one of my favorite songs on the album is, *He'll Find a Way* written by Babbie Mason. I was living in Tulsa but I wanted to go back to Georgia and work with Reid Hall again. Reid introduced me to a young lady who would profoundly affect my recording career from that day on. Cheryl Jones Rogers was an awarding winning arranger and producer who brought her professionalism to the album, and her talent to the production team.

Cheryl had a history of working with accomplished singers and musicians based out of Nashville, and as we began planning the new album, I quickly understood that she could help me reach a new level. Cheryl arranged every song and when she brought in her contacts such as Guy Penrod (formerly with the Gaither Vocal Band) and recording artist, Babbie Mason, the entire session became my most professional experience in a recording studio up to that time.

The revelation to me as an artist was just how comfortable and expressive Guy, Babbi, and the background singers were in a studio even when singing

214

alone. Up until that point in my recording career, I would stand in the recording booth behind a microphone and do my best to perfectly sing the song. I was very controlled and holding my body still as I referred to my sheet of music. But, when I watched Guy for the first time, I couldn't get over just how expressive and free he was in that little booth. It was as if he were singing in an auditorium full of thousands of listeners. He used his hands and moved as if he were communicating the song personally to an audience. Witnessing his technique and approach changed me for the better. People have commented to me regarding how I use my hands as I sing. After I watched those talented professionals it was as if I were given a license to perform in the studio the way I performed in front of an audience. Later in the session, Reid noticed the difference in me. It was the first time in a recording studio environment that I felt I was ministering in the presence of God.

Because Cheryl was such a gifted arranger, I asked her to put her touch on my signature song, *We Shall Behold Him*. Her ability to arrange the song was both comfortable and meaningful to me. She had a way of writing music that complimented my voice, and the song means even more to me now. Another song I selected for that album was *The Lord's Prayer*. It was a frequently requested song for me when I performed at weddings and I knew Cheryl could deliver something special as an arranger. When I think of the album, I think of how it was a transitional recording due to my growth as an artist. It was also a creative collaboration from start to finish that included a new freedom in my performances.

A few years later, I was privileged to work with Reid Hall again. I entitled my forth album, *In Christ Alone*. That album contains one of my most requested songs, *He'll Do it Again*. It also includes *Watch the Lamb, Your Grace and Mercy, Thank You,* and two of my most requested songs, *I Pledge Allegiance to the Lamb, The Anchor Holds.*

When I recorded album number five in Nashville, Tennessee, I got to work with my producer friend, Nathan DiGesare. I had no idea how personal this project would become until I was well into it. During production I received sad news that one of my pastor friends, Dr. Robert Griffin, of Parker Road Baptist Church in Florissant, Missouri, had just lost his wife, Gayle. Her passing really affected me emotionally and as I recorded the song, *Beyond*, I pictured her lovely face as I sang the words: *Beyond my eyes, beyond the skies, where tears turn to hope, and hope is the way of life. Beyond the realm of time and space, we'll see Jesus face-to-face.*

I was driving to one of my concerts as I heard the song, *Goodbye to Me* on my radio. I was so moved that I felt compelled to pull over on the shoulder of the highway so I could call the radio station for the details of the song. As I performed *Goodbye to Me* in my concerts it proved to be a reminder to my audiences and to me that we must die to ourselves each day so Jesus can work through us. Several songs on album five became concert favorites. The album includes: *I Bowed on My Knees, Midnight Cry, Jesus is the Answer, After the Rain, People Need the Lord, and Beyond.*

The cover of the album holds an interesting memory for me. Dying to self was a fitting theme to the album because it was something I had to do in order for

God to continue his work in me and through me. On the album cover, I am featured wearing a vest and white Nehru collared shirt. In the picture I have a stylish pin attached to the button on the collar of my shirt.

While ministering in England, I traveled to a church where the Lord allowed me to experience a life lesson I shall never forget. As I spoke with the pastor he shared with me a recent disappointment he had suffered while trying to book another American gospel singer. He had booked the "well-known" artist and the artist had a list of needs that had to be taken care of before he would perform.

He needed a first class ticket, a seat for his assistant who was accompanying him, a guaranteed number in the audience, as well as five thousand pounds in ticket sales. Five thousand pounds at that time was worth about nine thousand dollars. The pastor tried to raise enough funds, but he fell about a hundred and fifty pounds short of the goal. The singer refused to come until there was no shortfall.

As I listened to the pastor's story, I thought of all the times I had traveled and performed with no guarantees whatsoever. I simply went because God told me to go. However, I figured if this pastor had worked so hard for an artist who wouldn't show up, he must be going to really bless me financially for sacrificing so much to come to his fellowship.

It cost me fifty-five pounds to travel by train to his church, so you can imagine my reaction when after my concert he handed me fifty pounds and a handshake. In that moment, God was reminding me why the name of my album was, *Goodbye to Me*. The hurt I felt was tied to my needs being great. As a Christian artist and minister, I was looking to concerts to support my livelihood. It was hard to receive the fifty pounds with a pure and good heart. As I looked at the money, God told me to bless the pastor. I went to the pastor and I put twenty-five pounds in his hand and thanked him for allowing me to be a part of his ministry.

The lesson of *Goodbye to Me* continued. The youth pastor had commented earlier about how cool the pin was that was attached to my collar (the pin featured on the album cover). I took off the pin and I gave it to the youth pastor. I've learned over time that the best way to keep hurt from growing into bitterness is to sow the gift of love.

My sixth album that God allowed me to make was recorded just outside of Houston, Texas. I began to realize that each album had its unique meaning. What I thought would be another tool to bless, became a project full of personal significance as my family and I suffered through more challenges and trials.

While I was in Houston, one of my nephews, Brandon, was about to graduate from college. We were proud and preparing to celebrate his accomplishments. Brandon had made a profession of faith and I had heard him preach his first sermon. We received news that the vehicle in which he was traveling was involved in an accident, and my nephew was tragically killed. What made his death harder for me was the fact that we were looking forward to ministering together in the future.

Not long after that devastating event, my oldest brother, Dwight, lost his wife, Margie, to cancer. Margie was a well-loved pastor's wife full of caring and compassion. She was someone I could always talk to. My heart was so heavy, and I was filled with emotion as I attempted to sing in the studio. I asked God to take away the pain and hurt so I could perform well. I felt God saying; *Just worship Me right where you are.*

I thought back to Miss Georgia Tucker in our little Friendship Baptist church. She would tell us in her Sunday school class to count our blessings.

Count your blessings, name them one by one, and it will surprise you what the Lord has done.

The Nassau Bay was not far from where I was to record. It was peaceful and proved to be a place of inspiration as I sat pondering God's love through the sorrow. I prayed and had my devotion time with the Lord and I followed Miss Tucker's advice to count my blessings. I started with, *Thank you, Lord.* Before I knew it, my blessings turned into writing a song for Him. It goes like this:

In Your presence Lord, I stand trusting You to hold my hand, no matter what I'm going through I release my heart to You.

Thank You for Your love, O Lord, that strengthens me each day. Thank You for Your promise, to see You face-to-face.

Help me see the miracles that You perform each day. Help me see Your hand, O Lord, that guides me on my way.

I will serve no other god, my life is not my own. Jesus I want You to know my heart will be Your throne.

I will praise Your name, O Lord, for with You I'm not alone, and when I feel I'm weak, You tell me I am strong,

I will worship You, O Lord, I will worship you alone, I will worship You, O Lord, My heart will be Your throne. I will worship You, Jesus, I will worship You.

*Thank You for Your saving grace that freed me
from my sin, and for Your precious Holy Spirit that fills
me from within. Thank You for Your peace, O Lord, that
sets my heart at ease, You told me I could have it, Lord if
only I believed.*

I didn't set out to write a song, I just sat down to
write about what I was feeling during this time of
heartache. The album turned out to be a real treasure for
me despite the brokenness of that time. The songs on the
album are: *God is Good, Look What the Lord Has Done,
On Time God, Praise You Forever, You Are Great,
Honor and Glory, Draw Me Lord, Fill This Place, Holy,
Holy, Holy,* and *I Will Worship You.*

At the end of my time in Houston, I realized God
had taken me beyond the sadness and hurt and He had
blessed the project in unexpected ways.

For many years, supporters of my ministry
requested that I record a Christmas album so they might
enjoy it during the Christmas holiday season. It was my
pleasure to get into the recording studio to record my first
Christmas album titled, *It's Christmas Again.* The album
is especially close to my heart because God inspired me
to write five of the songs feature on the record. The
Christmas season has always meant a lot to my family
and me and expressing the truth of Christ's birth came
naturally as I wrote the songs. These first five songs are
the ones God gave me: *It's Christmas Again, Love Gives
Again and Again, Born A King, Sweet Was the Night, and
A Father's Heart.* The other songs on the album are:
*Silent Night, We Were the Reason, Mary Did You Know,
Oh Holy Night, Let There Be Peace on Earth.*

Predictably, *Mary Did You Know*, by Mark Lowry, is the most requested song I sing during the Christmas season. *It's Christmas Again* is also a favorite.

I teamed up with Cheryl Jones Rogers and Jeff Sandstrom in Atlanta to record my eighth album. There are several things about this recording experience that stands out to me all these years later. For one, I had chosen to record a beautiful song titled, *Fragrance of Christ*, by Babbie Mason. I asked Cheryl who she thought we could get to sing the duet with me.

"Why not Babbie?" she asked.

"Are you serious?" I replied.

"I'll ask her," Cheryl said.

Cheryl talked to Babbie and Babbie graciously said she would love to be a part of the recording. My family who lives in Atlanta came to the studio that day to meet Babbie and to witness my duet with a famous gospel singer. It was truly a red-letter day for my family and me. Babbie couldn't have been more thoughtful and warm. When she came to the studio I was so honored that she would take time out of her busy schedule to lay down the voice tracks with me. She told me it was her honor to be there with me.

Babbie arrived to the studio and I assumed that she would step into the booth, listen to the soundtrack, and record her vocals before mine.

"Let's sing this song together, Charles," Babbie said with a smile.

What an amazing moment. It all started with wanting to record one of Babbie's songs. Suddenly, I found myself in a recording studio singing a Babbie Mason song with Babbie Mason herself.

Fragrance of Christ quickly became one of my favorite songs. The other songs on that album were: *I Could Never Praise Him Enough, Nothing Else Matters, God is Good (All the Time), I Can Go to God in Prayer, It Doesn't Matter Who You Are, I Wish I Could, Never Give Up, Jesus is Love,* and *You Amaze Me.*

Regarding the album cover, my sisters, Joyce and Grace decided to take some control. They took me shopping in Atlanta and helped me pick out my wardrobe for the photo shoot. Thanks to my sisters and a good photographer, Zack Arias, I received lots of positive comments about the album cover.

The most requested songs off of my eighth album turned out to be *Nothing Else Matters* and *It Doesn't Matter Who you Are.* While visiting my brother-in-law, Jerry Gray, he asked me to listen to the song *Jesus is Love,* sung by Lionel Richie and the Commodores. The beauty of the song and the simplicity of the truth so moved me that I felt compelled to put it on the album. Audiences have enjoyed it for years. The song, *Never Give Up,* works really well with my teenaged audiences.

I was thrilled to have my ninth album, *Great is Thy Faithfulness,* co-produced by Cheryl Jones Rogers and Jeff Sandstrom. On that particular album I wanted to revisit and honor the hymns I had learned through my life. The old hymns of the churches had become more important to me as I got more involved with church work. I hadn't sung many hymns in my concerts to that point in my ministry, but I had always found a great deal of strength in them and enjoyed singing them.

As we produced Cheryl's arrangements, it was important to me to add some choir voices to a few of the songs. The choirs I asked to join us were from Eastside

222

Baptist Church in Marietta, Georgia, directed by music minister Darrell Whipple, and the Royal Baptist Church in Newnan, Georgia, directed by their music minister Billy Jack Green. I knew the directors and I knew their terrific choirs would add beautifully to the album.

Perhaps the most amazing thing that happened to us during the *Great is Thy Faithfulness* project was when I gave Cheryl the task of arranging a song that could include the singing voices of the children from the New Hope orphanage in Burundi. There was a group of students I had watched grow up and I had heard them sing in the past. In my head I could hear them singing the old hymn, *How Firm a Foundation*, and I became committed to doing whatever it would take to have them featured on that song. Cheryl arranged the choral part and I sent the music to my friend in Burundi who agreed to teach the kids their part of the song. The children in the orphanage were thrilled at the prospect of singing and being recorded for my newest album.

I flew to Africa and the twenty students gathered with me in Bujumbura, Burundi. We arrived at the studio at 10 a.m. and that's when I learned that the city had rolling blackouts. In other words, the government would choose what parts of town received electricity and what parts wouldn't receive it for periods of time during the day. Unfortunately for us, on the day that we had chosen to record, the studio was in the section of the city with no power. No one was sure when electricity would be turned back on.

To make matters worse, it was an extremely hot day with temperatures over one hundred degrees. Even if we had power to record, the place where we were to sing and record didn't have air conditioning. In fact, the studio didn't even have windows to allow in any breeze.

The long, hot hours crawled by and still there was no power. The engineer assured me that power could eventually return, but when 1:00 p.m. rolled around, I ordered food and fed the children, unsure if they would get to sing. More hours passed and at 5:00 p.m. I told them it was time to get back to the orphanage. The kids protested and begged to stay, assuring me that the power would come back on any moment.

"We will wait!" they shouted.

We waited and waited until 8:00 p.m. approached. We had been there ten hours and there was no power in sight. Just as we were about to call it off, the power came on in the room!

The children cheered and we were so excited to get the chance to perform and record. The room was still steamy hot, but the kids took their places and the engineer sat behind the crude and dated engineering console, ready to capture their voices.

The Burundian students sang beautifully in their native tongue of Karundi, and they blessed my heart. Their first take was a "keeper" despite the children having to survive all day in the heat before they performed. We were at the end of a very long and tiring day, but I don't think we could have done any better had we used the best state-of-the-art studio in the United States. God heard our prayers and answered them.

We downloaded the track on a thumb drive and I guarded it with my life all the way back to Georgia where I personally handed it to Cheryl. When Jeff and Cheryl played back the voices of the Burundian children, they sat in amazement. It was breathtaking.

The songs chosen for my ninth album were: *Great is Thy Faithfulness, The Love of God, Abide With Me, Lighthouse, Amazing Grace, He Looked Beyond My Faults, I Choose to Worship, How Firm a Foundation, If I Can Help Somebody, Let the Church Say Amen,* and *Find Us Faithful.*

Traveling the world and singing for the Lord has been a privilege and honor for me. Being able to capture in recordings the music of some of gospel's greatest writers and performers has provided for me many of the true highlights of my life. As a boy, I would listen to my tiny transistor radio and wonder what it would be like to hear my voice across the airwaves. God knew my desires because he had placed them in my heart. Becoming a recording artist was a fulfillment of one of my childhood dreams.

CHAPTER 17

"The Fountains"

Sometimes, it is hard for me to believe that I lived a quarter of a century in the communities of Temecula and Murrieta, California. When I was a child in Arkansas, living in California hadn't crossed my mind, but it was certainly a state I had dreamed about visiting. I wrote earlier that during my days at Rhema Bible Training Center in Broken Arrow, Oklahoma, I had the privilege of meeting a man and his wife who would profoundly impact my life. Pastor Roger Brewer and his wife, Evelyn Brewer, felt a calling to Southern California, and the Lord led them to the dusty western cowboy town of Temecula. After graduation from Rhema I followed Pastor Roger out there because his spiritual influence on me was so strong that I wished for his continued teaching and guidance. In fact, when I went to minister with them for the first time in California, I knew in my heart that I was supposed to walk alongside them until God told me otherwise.

I should explain that my introduction to California was a far cry from the wonderful images I had seen or envisioned for me on the West Coast. In my mind, I was traveling to the sunny beaches of Southern California, where all I would see was palm trees, beautiful sunsets, and movie stars. However, what I got as I drove into town was the smell of sheep and cattle and hay as I followed a farmer into the sleepy little town of Temecula.

The buildings were right out of a John Wayne movie, and there were less than four thousand persons living there. I left southeast Arkansas's farmland and ended up in California's version of a Southern rural farm community. Temecula wasn't incorporated as a city when I arrived. Old Town was just that—an old western town built with wooden structures located near the Pechanga Indian Reservation.

"Pastor, are you sure the Lord has called you to Temecula? There are more cows and sheep than there are people," I commented.

"This is where God has called me, Charles," he assured me.

The first time some members of my family came out to visit me in California, they had the same reaction.

"You sure this is California?"

The first thing they noticed was the large amount of livestock everywhere. Following farmers hauling hay was what I left behind in Arkansas, and it was the first thing to greet me in my new home in California. What a shock to my system. I was in California, and it felt as if I were back in Arkansas.

One of the things that made my transition to Temecula a more comfortable one was the fact that Roger and Evie had agreed to let me live with them and serve in the ministry as the new church began. New Covenant Church had a very humble beginning. First, we met in a home, and as the months and years passed, we met in storefronts, movie theaters, schools, renovated warehouses, and finally a newly constructed church campus.

In January of 1989, I began my official position with New Covenant Church. My primary role was to serve the pastors in any capacity needed. I led the music service, functioned for a time as youth pastor, and participated in any other role in which Pastor Roger needed me, but all the while my main ministry was to travel all over the world to sing and preach God's Word.

Because travel got into my blood, it was no big deal for me to get in my vehicle and go anywhere. I operate that way still today. It's not unusual for me to drop everything to officiate a funeral one day in Florida and then minister in a church in California a couple of days later. My family has gotten used to asking where I am in the world, and that has been a wonderful part of God's calling on my life. Because of the way of life I have chosen, the world has become smaller.

When I moved to Temecula, California, I acted as if Los Angeles was just a short trip across town. In reality, it was a two, to three-hour journey on the road, depending on traffic. When my friends came to visit California, they would want to see all the iconic tourist destinations, and Temecula was not on the list.

"I'm meeting friends for breakfast," I told Pastor Roger.

"Where you headed?"

"Hollywood," I said, as if going down the street.

It was very common to meet friends on Hollywood Boulevard in front of the Grauman's Chinese Theater. I was never more connected to the city of L.A. than when I drove down a street in Beverly Hills to see the majestic palm trees lining my way. The sun, palm trees, and mansions helped me to feel as though I had "made it" to California.

Temecula is a forty-minute drive to the Pacific Ocean, so in reality I didn't have to go very far to get the real California experience. I may have lived near the sheep and cattle, but every day I had the Pacific coast at my disposal. It was extremely relaxing to drive up or down the coast and spend time talking and communing with God. There will always be something powerful about standing on the beach at the edge of a continent to observe the wonder of our Creator.

It didn't take very long for me to understand why God had called Pastor Roger to the dusty little town of Temecula. It seemed as though overnight the town grew from 4,000 people to 110,000 citizens right before our eyes. Temecula and its sister city to the north, Murietta, began growing together. Murietta was small when I shopped for my first home there. Today the population is over 103,000. Combining Temecula's 110,000 with Murietta's population, one can quickly see that Pastor Roger's calling from God was clear and had an obvious purpose.

Purchasing a home was a huge step of faith because I hadn't owned a home until that time. Pastors Roger and Evie and I visited new housing construction and enjoyed going into the model homes. New home starts were happening daily, and to entice buyers to move out to the country some of the builders were giving away a Mercedes with a purchase!

During this time of rapid expansion, a gentleman in our church named Bill informed me that he had a condo that he would like me to own. The condominium was a two-bedroom home set on a hill. It was an older unit that had been one of the first constructed in the subdivision. I was informed later that actor Don Ameci was one of the investors.

When I thought seriously about moving into the condo, I noticed that I would be in a community that was mostly retired persons living out their golden years next to a beautiful golf course. It might go without saying, but I must mention that I was the only African-American living in the predominately white neighborhood full of private people. Of course, I was all about being proactive and making new friends. The first person I met was Mrs. Bartlett, an elderly widow who walked her dog daily to the mailbox. She was very sweet and seemed more than willing to become my friend. She would bake cookies and proudly share them with me. After lots of mailbox and cookie meetings I felt as though I knew a lot about her and she knew a lot about me. She told me of her nephew who lived in Gallup, New Mexico, so during one of my drives from California back to Arkansas, I decided to exit at Gallup and track down Mrs. Bartlett's nephew. When I walked into the nephew's store and I told him that he and I had a mutual friend, I believe I caught him off guard. It took a few minutes, but he relaxed once he realized who my neighbor was. Through the years I have made it a point to stop in Gallup to say hello.

One Sunday morning, I invited Mrs. Bartlett to attend church with me. She was attending a more conservative church with her son and daughter-in-law at the time. I drove her to church that morning, and I had some reservations because our church tended to be rather loud with instruments and praise worship. During the service, I noticed she was happy and clapping along with the music. It took me by surprise.

"It seemed as if you enjoyed yourself at the service today, Mrs. Bartlett," I told her.

"I did. Your church is more like the one I attended back home. It's the kind I grew up in, and I loved it!" she assured me with a smile.

One morning during the first rolling earthquake I experienced while living in the new neighborhood, my first instinct was to go check on the welfare of Mrs. Bartlett. I ran to her house and knocked on her door. She calmly opened the door.

"Are you okay?" I asked with concern.

"Oh, honey, I've lived through so many earthquakes they don't bother me at all," she laughed.

"Oh. Well, next time it happens, maybe you should check on me!" I replied.

Jim and Clara were a lovely couple living across the cul-de-sac from me. They were familiar to the neighborhood and I quickly learned that Jim was the self-appointed neighborhood watch person. He approached me a few weeks after meeting him.

"You know, everyone has been talking," he stated with little emotion.

I had a pretty good idea what he meant. I was the new black man who had moved in and I had become the talk of the neighborhood.

With a serious look on his face, Jim continued, "I told the neighbors I'd rather have ten of you than one white person."

"Thank you, Jim. That means a lot to me."

Jim walked back to his home, and a good feeling swelled up inside me. His awkward but genuine attempt at making me feel welcome will never be forgotten. It was the beginning of a very good friendship. As I hosted my missionary friends, Curt and Valerie, they shared the gospel with Jim, and he accepted Jesus as his personal Savior.

Jim was genuinely interested in where I was going across the world and he enjoyed the recaps of my adventures when I returned. Jim also took it upon himself to police my house when I was gone. One day, my friend Bob came to retrieve some of his belongings he had temporarily stored in my garage. Thanks to Jim, the police showed up to question Bob about being in my house.

On another occasion, my friend Dale came to my condo to install a washing machine for me. Jim put a ladder in front of the door and pretended to be fixing the porch light so when Dale exited the house, he would have to engage Jim in conversation. Once he had a chance to interrogate Dale, Jim picked up his ladder and walked back home. Awkward moments by Jim were a testimony of his devotion to our friendship, and his commitment to watch over my home when I was gone.

I had lots of adventures in that new condo in Murietta. One night that stands out in my mind is the night I lost my house key, and I was forced to devise a plan to break into my own house without being detected. Knowing that people like Jim would be checking out their windows periodically, I had to carefully figure out how I could "with stealth" get past their watchful eyes. There happened to be a small kitchen window I could force open that would be out of sight and would allow me to quietly crawl into my house. As I wriggled through the window and then slid awkwardly across the butcher-block table, staring me in the face was a strange business card. It seems that my neighbor, Jim, had called the police while I was out of town, and the local police had been there sometime before I broke into my own condo. They had come in my house to inspect it and to make sure I hadn't been robbed. It is humorous to me still as I remember back to breaking in my own house and recall stretching headlong across my butcher-block table reading that business card from our local police. Ironically, no one saw me break in.

Having neighbors and friends on my cul-de-sac like Jim and Clara, Tony and Cindy, a young man named Chris, and sweet Mrs. Bartlett, was just what I needed at the time. Years later when I heard Jim had passed away, the memories of his unique friendship came rushing back to me. What an honor it was to preside over his funeral, knowing that my dear neighbor and I would someday be reunited in Heaven, where we would be neighbors again.

For twenty-five years, California was my home. Ministry time in California included the beginning of a new church and all that goes with that. In those early days I just met needs of the church, working in the music department and helping to establish it. My job depended on what needs there were in the church. It could vary between leading youth, leading music, or preaching. I might even find myself building, painting, and cleaning the church. I was there to do whatever God wanted me to do. It was at that church that I learned what it was like to be engaged in the lives of people on a weekly basis, not like the itinerate ministry I had done in the past.

A trait from my Southern upbringing that I found beneficial was my outgoing personality. It was easy for me to meet people in public and I felt comfortable inviting them to our church. Because Pastor Roger's background was in horse training, he and I would go minister at the horse training facility. We would hold

Bible studies, and I would sing for the workers. When I ended our time together in prayer, the men would often ask me to pray that they would get a green card. Innocently, I would pray that they would get a green card, and after the prayer, I would invite them to our new church. I told them that I would gladly come back on Sunday morning and give them a ride if they were willing to attend our church. To my surprise, every one of the workers agreed to come to church. I was excited to share the good news with Pastor Roger that my evangelism outreach at the horse training center had paid off. Pastor Roger gently took me aside and said,

"Charles, if they are asking you to pray that they get a green card that means they aren't legal citizens yet. You could be arrested for transporting them to church."

We continued ministering to the men, but we kept our activities at the training facilities. Fortunately, I saw several get saved and many received their green cards.

One morning, the pastor's wife, Evie, told me she had sent my music album to the Trinity Broadcasting Network, a Christian television station. She received a positive response from them and they requested that I come to the studio and sing on one of their programs. I was excited at the prospect of being on television.

Immediately my mind went to what I would sing and what I would wear. It was the days of the navy double-breasted jackets and gray slacks. Choosing what to wear was easy, but choosing the song to sing required more prayer. I settled on the song *We Shall Behold Him*, one of my favorites. I practiced much of the day, and then traveled from Temecula to Tustin, California. It was exciting to drive up to the studio and be given a parking pass by the gate attendant. I parked my blue van, Genesis, and I walked into the studio where I was met by the program director. I was escorted to the performing area and for me it was a surreal moment to be standing on the spot where I had seen other gospel singers perform. To my surprise, Dottie Rambo, the artist who had written the song I was to perform, was a guest on the show that night. Because it was too late to change the song, I sang *We Shall Behold Him* with her sitting and watching me. When I finished singing, I heard the show host, Paul Crouch, Sr., ask Mrs. Rambo how it makes her feel when she hears other artists sing her songs.

"They become my children," she replied as she looked my way.

Later, I had the chance to visit with her. She was very sweet and encouraging to me. It was an honor to be standing in the presence of such an anointed gospel artist, and I was humbled by her kind words.

The following evening I was scheduled to sing a song called *He is Jehovah*, and the person who had written that song, Betty Jean Robinson, was a guest on the show. I'm not sure what God was saying to me, but it was a privilege I will never forget. I was also honored to make the acquaintance of one of America's premier preachers, Dr. E.V. Hill.

Other memories of my time in California include being asked to pray at city council meetings and receiving a note saying that my prayer had to be a non-sectarian prayer. The only way I knew to pray to God was in the name of Jesus. I am pleased to say they invited me back several times.

After I returned from a trip overseas, Pastor Roger and Evie picked me up at the Los Angeles Airport. During the ride home they asked if I would take the position of youth pastor because the present pastors were heading to Bible school. They asked me to pray about it and after several months I finally responded to their request. I didn't feel that God had told me specifically to be a youth pastor, but I did know the Lord had spoken to me to serve and meet the needs of the church. I said if that was where they needed me to serve I would gladly do it.

Pastor Roger and Evie gave me permission to continue traveling and ministering while serving as the church's part-time youth pastor. It wasn't long before I discovered the needs of the youth were so great they needed a full-time youth pastor, not a part-time. Because of that great need, I had to come off the road and serve the kids and their families each week.

Pastor Roger and Evie had dedicated their lives to serving the Lord, and I was blessed to be a part of that journey, but our time doing ministry together was coming to an end. When they retired, I felt a release that it was time for me to make a bold move as well. My role up to that point was to serve and support Pastors Roger and Evie and the other ministers at New Covenant, but when the new pastors, Gary and Anne Martin became the leaders of the church, I was honored to be asked to continue serving on the board.

Suddenly, it seemed God was calling me to another path although I didn't have a clear direction as to what the path was. The initial exploration to find God's will for my life came when Reverend Bob Gordon invited me to serve on staff at his Bible school in the United Kingdom. While in Scotland I earnestly sought out the call of God. I understood in my spirit that God wanted me to continue ministering in the United Kingdom, but not full-time in the Bible school.

I flew back to California and continued praying and searching for God's guidance. I went to Nashville, thinking I would find a place in and around Christian artists there, but I didn't have a peace about it once I got there. I went back to Missouri, where I knew that there were many potential opportunities to serve in ministry, but again I had no peace about it. Next, I went to Atlanta, but just as I had found in Missouri, there was a lot of love and opportunity for ministry, but no peace about going there.

I learned that when I seek direction and an answer from the Lord, I should stay planted where I am until I get the answer. I went back to California and prayed, "Lord, you will show me." I rested in that.

Later that year, it was time to go home to Dermott, Arkansas, to visit my family. As I had done hundreds of times over the decades, I casually drove through town. There was a group of men who gathered around a tree each day to talk about the world and try to solve all its problems. On previous occasions I would wave at them and keep traveling toward home, but during this particular visit something was very different. I genuinely looked at the group of men at the tree, and when they waved back to me with friendly smiles; it was as if I were seeing their faces for the first time. The Lord spoke His clear direction to my spirit and said,

I'm bringing you home.

When I arrived at my house, I could hear those words in my spirit. Believe me, it was the last thing I expected to hear from God. When I eagerly left my family and home in 1975, it was as if I had made a solemn pledge to myself that I would never live in Arkansas again. As long as my family was living there, it was a place to visit on occasion, that was the vow to me.

"I'm bringing you home." Those words kept ringing in my thoughts. I would say the words captivated my mind as I instantly began looking at the community in a different way. During that visit I didn't share with my family what God had told me. As I drove back to California, I had lots of time on the road to prayerfully consider what God said.

Several months later, back in California, my phone rang and my brother Stanley was on the other line.

"Hey, Charles, you'll never believe what's for sale."

"What is it?" I inquired.

"The big house at Baxter."

My heart leaped a bit as I immediately pictured the house, the barns, and the land on the property where my family had worked the fields.

The weeks passed, but when I arrived back in Arkansas on my next visit to see family, I drove directly to the property to take a close look at it. I pulled into the driveway, and I sat quietly in my vehicle. I inspected all of the property I could see, and I asked the Lord,

"…If you are bringing me home, is this a part of my journey?"

But that moment in the driveway would not be my last. For the next year as I visited my family, I would go to the property, park in the driveway, and talk with the Lord about His will for my life. Eventually, I called a realtor to find out the particulars about the house and what was for sale around it. After I gathered more information, my next step was to share what I had learned with my mother.

"I'm praying about buying the property at Baxter," I told her.

"That would be wonderful, Charles."

"It needs to be a secret between you and me. A lot of things would need to line up, and I'm still praying and considering it," I reminded her.

Mother could keep a secret, and I liked having someone I could tell. It took about a year and a half, however, before I got to a point where I could share it with my whole family. The reaction was a positive one for many reasons, but the bottom line for the family was that I would be moving back home.

The road back home wasn't simple, and there were many things that had to come together, not the least of which was for me to secure the property. During another trip back I arranged for a realtor to meet me at the farmhouse so I could go inside and give it an initial inspection. She told me the house was on the market, and the sellers included seventeen acres with the house, the barn, and several outbuildings.

Imagine the thoughts rushing through my mind when I parked in the driveway and stepped out of my vehicle. All the years that had passed since I worked in the fields were a blur. My mind raced back to my childhood when I stood in the cotton and bean fields behind the house. My family and I had worked the fields for many hours to keep us fed. As I stood there, I saw the majestic Dutch barn to the right and a horse-riding arena straight ahead. I looked to see the old bell that would ring and call workers to and from the fields. As I looked at the bell, I vowed to myself that if I owned this property, the bell would ring for happy occasions or just for fun, not for work demands. The sound of that bell had to have a new purpose.

The house, built in the early 1900's, had not been lived in for many years and was desperate for modern renovations. The entire property had major needs due to recent neglect. But I saw its potential.

"What's included in the seventeen acres?" I asked.

The agent looked around, and I could tell she wasn't quite sure. After a moment, she assured me that she would do her due diligence and get back to me regarding property dimensions, as well as determine what buildings near the farm were included. After my brief inspection, I stepped back into my vehicle and took a deep breath. Before I drove away, I prayed, and I dreamed about what it might look like to actually occupy the land.

Some time passed as I continued my ministering around the world, but all the while I couldn't get the thought of relocating back to Arkansas out of my mind. I picked up the telephone and placed a call to Jerry, the owner, to gather more information about the property. Jerry was very open as he told me that his father, the previous owner, was alive and living on the west side of the property, where he was still raising bulls and cattle. In fact, they were grazing up to the edge of the property near the house. It was during this conversation that I got the disappointing news that he was not in a position to sell the house with seventeen acres, but rather the house and only six acres. Even though I was presently living in a house in California that sat on a little parcel of land where one could reach out the window and almost shake hands with the neighbor, settling for six acres was not what I wanted to do. Previously, a friend had given me advice that rang in my ears:

"Because God isn't making any more land, get as much as you can the first time."

I informed Jerry that if the situation were to change I would be a potential buyer of the property including the house, and if the seventeen acres became available again, I requested he call me. All the while, I kept thinking about how six acres would have been a dream property in California. However, if I were to return home and develop the property into a special place of ministry, I would need more room to expand the vision.

Six months later the phone rang and it was Jerry calling to inform me that his father had passed away.

"Charles, I'd like to talk to you about the property," he informed me.

I offered him my condolences regarding his father's death and assured him that I was still interested in discussing my purchase of the property if the terms and conditions were agreeable. He told me that we could talk about the details the next time I came home. Several weeks later we arranged to meet at the house. Because God was in control, I had no reason to be nervous or concerned about it.

"Charles, the property is still for sale. Would you be interested in the house and one hundred acres?" Jerry asked.

Once again, God was showing me that His plans are always better than I could imagine. Jerry explained the boundaries of the one hundred acres. It included the house, five barns, three smaller buildings, a pecan orchard, and nearly eighty acres of pastureland. Also included in the property was the easement to Bayou Bartholomew. I could have never imagined that I would be given the opportunity to own the easement where I was baptized as a ten-year-old.

I knew I would need a realtor to assist me with the purchase and a dear realtor friend of mine named Becky came to mind. She was living in Little Rock, Arkansas at that time, and I knew in my heart she was the one to help me. Her life was connected with mine in a distant way during our early years in Dermott. Becky's mother lived in Dermott, and it was her mother's sister that my mother used to cook for. When I used to go into the office in town to pay a utility bill, it was Becky's mother, Mrs. Jean, who would greet me at the counter.

"Charles Graham, when I die, I want you to sing at my funeral," Mrs. Jean would say.

I would make a humorous remark and then assure her that if she didn't outlive me, it would be my honor to sing at her funeral. Years later, I had just landed from ministering in England when I got a call from Becky. She introduced herself and then informed me that her mother had died, and it was her mom's request that I sing at the funeral service. I got in my vehicle and headed to Arkansas to fulfill Mrs. Jean's wish. From the moment I met Becky until this day, we have remained good friends. Her grandchildren have called me "Uncle Charles" for years, and God knew long ago that Becky and I were destined to be friends. I was aware that Becky was a realtor in Arkansas, so I felt I had an advocate who would work for me as I began the process of purchasing the property.

What should have been a fairly quick real estate transaction became much longer in its duration. Having given the entire situation to the Lord, I had already decided that God would be in control of it all, and not me. In the middle of the process of buying the property, I was given an opportunity to minister in Estonia. I stayed on the ministry path and left for Europe in the middle of negotiations. I gave Becky permission to continue to negotiate for me as I was away doing my ministry work. The enemy said to me that it would not be wise to walk away from the situation when I did, but I knew if God held the property for me all those years, He would keep it for me as I was away.

Becky and I stayed in touch, and it became a walk and journey of faith for her and me. She ran into some obstacles while I was in Estonia, and I reminded her that all difficulties we encountered during negotiations and transactions we would approach with peace. As God would have it, when I arrived back from Estonia, I signed the agreement, and the property was officially secured in my name. My name may have been written on all the papers and official documents, but I knew like no one else that the name on the deed was "God, My Father." Standing in that surreal moment, I realized I was at an intersection of my life. As a boy I could only walk past the house, and decades later I was privileged to live in it.

My next prayerful thought was, *What should I name this place*? While I did not know all of what God wanted to do with the property, this I did know; it was to be a place where those in ministry could come and receive rest and ministry in their lives—thus the name *The Fountains: A Place of Refreshing*. A pastor friend from England, Tom Thompson, and his wife, Rosemary, were visiting me at the property, and they shared a scripture verse referencing The Fountains. Revelation:

21:6 says: "And he said unto me, it is done. I am Alpha and Omega, the beginning and the end. I will give unto him that is athirst of the fountain of the water of life freely."

When I consider God's miracles that have led me to this day, I often ponder the moments in my life when He provided for me and sustained me financially. I would like to believe that I am light years away from my Bible school days, when my roommate, Joe, and I were combining and counting our coins to try to buy a meal, but living by faith as I do, I'm learning there are always challenges. When I wake up in the morning and I know a bill is due but there is no money to make the payment, God gives me peace. He has taught me, what I need more than the provision is the assurance that He is by my side giving me peace before I see the provision.

There were times when I had to back off my plans of making improvements at the property. I had to delay projects and overcome the temporary embarrassments, such as the steps to the front door not being completely painted. I learned to remain grateful and minister with what I had while continually asking God to bless and honor it. I'm happy to report that He has never failed me.

The road to maturity is not an overnight process. Through the purchase process He reinforced many times the truth that peace precedes provision. God taught me that He is my provider, not people. He made it clear on many occasions that He wanted me to have peace, and not just because the finances were there, but because He was there. There were times when I went to the cupboard and just like "Old Mother Hubbard's" cupboard, my cabinet was bare. As we would say in Arkansas: *There ain't nothin'!* There were times when I just had enough to fix a cup of tea. It was the Lord and me during those times. What He wanted from me was my love and trust in Him. There was an understanding that had to be established in my mind and in my spiritual maturity. He wanted me to know that it was my Father providing for me and no one else. Through that teaching, He also wanted me to learn that I must give. The story of the widow who gave the widow's mite always comes to my mind. God didn't force that gift out of her. She freely gave what she had, and in her case she gave ALL she had.

Learning to trust God in the area of finances proved beneficial as I approached the time to address all the needs of the property. At the time I purchased the house, it had been empty for years and was in a sad state of deterioration. There were boards hanging, and much like an old abandoned house, it was hard to imagine that any amount of reconstruction could bring the old place back to life.

What encouraged me daily was the fresh approach that God had planted in my mind. As we moved forward on the renovation of the house, my concerns would not be based on its physical appearance or the mountain of extreme needs. All I needed to proceed was a confirmation from God that my purchase of the property was part of His perfect plan.

I surveyed the work that had to be done on the property with friends who had construction backgrounds. Darryl Coons and Leon Gregory conducted the preliminary analysis of what had to be repaired and in what order the work should be done. First, the house needed a new roof. That's when I became aware of what the pros mean by a top-down renovation. A good roof would protect everything below it.

Besides the roof, the exterior of the farmhouse had severely deteriorated wooden trim that was in dire need of replacement as well. Below the trim the sturdy brick walls were in decent condition. The rest of the home's wooden structures such as porches, and their support columns, had to be addressed.

A project the size and scope of The Fountains cannot be tackled alone. I knew that fact when the Lord made a way for its purchase. Because the project was so much bigger than me and so far out of the realm of my knowledge and skills, I knew God would have to send people of expertise my way.

Darryl and Leon orchestrated and organized the project as if they were in the prime of their careers. They didn't just bark orders; they got in there and personally climbed, hammered, and sawed as they led the transformation of the farmhouse. More construction help came from my friends, British pastors, Myra and Allister Lewis. I had ministered in their church on occasion, and they came to the United States for an extended time to help with renovation of The Fountains.

Adding to that help was a crew from Newnan, Georgia. Another reminder of how God was planning it long before I even understood His will for my life, my friend of forty years, Billy Jack Green, gave me a call. When he heard about The Fountains, he called to see if his church, Royal Baptist Church in Newnan, could make The Fountains their ministry project for the year. Each summer the church sought out projects for members of their congregation–from retired persons down to young children. Billy Jack brought nearly forty people to work and stay on the property for a week. That was in the earliest days of the renovation, and their builders, electricians, welders, plumbers, and painters had plenty to do, and they did it well. The crew from Georgia also cleared the orchard and the land of debris. They burned trash and made an instant difference to the look of the farmhouse property.

After the purchase of the property, I prayed about my neighbors and asked God for good relationships between us. It was refreshing to be approached by such friendly people and it was a good feeling to know my next-door neighbors were good Christian brothers. My new neighbor, Sam, had told his mother about the large crew of people who had come in for the week of work. As the workers were busy around the house, a white SUV arrived in the driveway and a lady got out and introduced herself as Ann Whitaker, the mother of Sam and Jim Whitaker, the men who farmed the land next to The Fountains. Sam and Jim's mother wanted to show the crew some Southern hospitality, and as a result, Mrs. Ann's church baked and prepared delicious desserts and cookies for my guest workers.

The interior of the farmhouse was in good condition as far as structural soundness. Contractors today would say it has "good bones." There was an electrical issue with wiring, so wall sconces, outlets, switches, and fixtures had to be replaced and updated to modern codes. The walls were strong shiplap boards covered with old wallpaper. The paper was peeling off, and to make the walls work, we would have to hang sheetrock throughout the entire house. The good news was that newly covered walls would give me a fresh palette to add whatever colors and textures I desired to the walls.

Because I didn't want to compromise the character of the house, especially the crown molding, I had the electricians carefully rewire without hurting the older features of the house.

A priority for me, regarding how my guests would be accommodated, was to have private bathrooms in each bedroom, which meant there would have to be two new bathrooms designed, plumbed, and constructed. Converting the two sleeping porches added two more bedrooms to the house, giving me seven bedrooms total. The side porch and back porch were converted into comfortable sitting rooms.

Ron and Karen, my pastor friends out of Chicago, came to visit and inspect my floors. To my excitement, Pastor Ron discovered that under all the rugs and old carpet were hardwood floors crying out for restoration. In his opinion, the wood was in good shape and could be brought back to life. When he was finished with the sanding and refinishing process, the floors were restored to their original beauty.

The sole purpose of owning such a large house was for hosting people, and it is near-impossible to host people without a fully-functioning, modernized kitchen. Much of the ministry of Jesus is centered on food and its importance, and I wanted the kitchen to be a place to gather, to visit, and to find nourishment.

So we completely gutted the room. My crew and I pulled out everything, including the cabinets and countertops, and we freshened up the room with new walls, new ceiling, new cabinets, granite countertops, an island in the middle of the room, and, thanks to my brother Willie, new tile floors.

One of my greatest desires for the kitchen was for it to feature a farm sink. There is a dear artist friend of mine from Oklahoma, who wanted to do something special for the farm and our new ministry. Wantha is an accomplished craftsperson who paints beautiful things on ceramic, so when she asked me what I would like painted on the farm sink I told her I would leave that to her divine inspiration.

During her first attempt to paint and fire the farm sink in her kiln, it cracked. She attempted the firing a second and a third time, and each time her sinks cracked. One day she called, and the disappointment in her voice was apparent.

"I am so sorry, Charles. I've tried three times, and each time the sink has cracked."

Having been an artist, I understood intimately the discouragement one can feel when art doesn't turn out as planned.

"Does it leak?" I asked.

"No, it's just a hairline crack," she replied, "but I don't want to give you something that's cracked."

I thought for moment and was convinced that her art was supposed to be in The Fountains just as it was.

"Jesus has scars, so I don't have a problem with scars if it is functioning," I assured her.

When the sink arrived, I saw the stunning art she had created. She had painted a beautiful picture of a variety of fruits, similar to a horn of plenty. What she didn't know was one of my favorite scriptures is Galatians 5:22, the fruit of the Spirit. On the inside of the sink, she had inscribed "His bread, His water, His Spirit, freely He gave, freely you receive."

The sink ended up being a treasure for The Fountains and a delight to everyone who has visited. The kitchen became the most renovated part of the house with new appliances and features, and it is a room that I cherish because of the fellowship and conversations that happen in that space.

When I look out my kitchen window, I see the beautiful orchard where I used to pick pecans to make extra money as a boy. I thank God that something as simple as an orchard has become part of my story. As I write this book, I have big plans for the pecan orchard. Recently, we had a wedding in the orchard, and I received word not long ago from my former pastor that the old church where my family and I attended is no longer in use. He told me that he prayed, and God told him to give me the church. I graciously accepted the offer, and the old Friendship Baptist Church is set to be moved to the pecan orchard, where it will be known as Friendship Chapel at The Fountains. I'm excited about what God will do with the new facility on my property.

Just a short walk from the back door of the house is the Dutch barn that many people in my community remember from their past. I have heard comments from a variety of people, young and old, who share with me their memories of the barn. The structure is very efficient in its design, and it stands not only as a testament of the wealth of the man who built it, but also an example of how the farmer took care of his animals. The Dutch barn and other barns at The Fountains have served as beautiful backdrops for weddings and school pictures.

There is also a large horse-riding arena that was built in the 1960's. The structure, with its steel trusses and large square footage, is the building that I intend to renovate into an all-purpose facility for retreats, reunions, and ministry gatherings. I want it to be a dedicated meeting space for education and for ministry.

The workers from different states and countries made quite an impression on the people of my community. One day I walked into my local bank, and the bank president called me aside.

"How did you get all those white people to come and work for you?" he asked me.

"It's a family thing," I replied.

We both laughed as I left the building.

When the work was done, I remember the comment I made to Billy Jack that I knew God would use them to bless the ministry, but I prayed that He would use them to bless the community as well. I asked all the pastors in town to bring their wives and their congregations out for a reception at The Fountains so they could be some of the first to see the transformation. As we all stood there together, I could see that God had answered that prayer completely. Never was the scripture in the Gospel of Matthew more evident in my community to:

"Let your light so shine before others, that they may see your good deeds and glorify your Father in Heaven."

Remember the old bell behind the house—the large bell that was used to bring the farmhands in from the field? When I committed to refurbishing the beautiful old house, I made a pledge that the first time that bell would ring under my ownership it would be rung for a moment of celebration. The first event on the calendar was my mother's seventy-fifth birthday. What a joy it was to hear the resounding tone when the bell rang out its first sounds as part of The Fountains property.

Traditionally, the sound of a bell ringing marked time. Often the clanging tones would mark the beginning or the end of a workday. At The Fountains, the bell would not be sounded as a remembrance of time in the past, but rather a clarion call to take us all from hurts of history into the healing time of our future. For me, the bell would never again serve to remind me of racial separation, but it would serve to remind me that God can and will conquer and heal my hurts.

Today, as I walk among the people of my community, I realize that some of the people were here when I was a boy. I'm thankful to know that I'm not walking in the hurt, but I am free to be both friend and brother to my community. Only God could have known how full my heart could be when free from hurts and free to love. People often say,

What an amazing story to own the house you weren't able to enter and to own the easement to the bayou where you were baptized.

I have to remind them that the real story was that God trusted me to come home to love all of the community. Never was that more apparent than the day the doorbell rang and I saw a young man who introduced himself to me as someone I had known as a young boy. I welcomed the young man into the home in which he used to live.

"My dad told me I had to come out to see what you have done to the place," he said.

The young man was Steven. He escorted his girlfriend, Barbara, through the house, and he complimented me about all the changes. Steven showed Barbara his old bedroom and the sleeping porch. He remarked that he rarely walked out on that porch. We finished the tour, and he thanked me. Before Steven and Barbara left to return home to Texas, I gave them one of my music CDs.

A few days later, I received a phone call, and Steven told me how much they enjoyed the CD. Then, he gave me the big news that he had asked Barbara to marry him. After she said "yes," he asked her what she thought would be her ideal wedding. Barbara said she would love to go back to Arkansas and get married where he grew up. She said she would like Brother Charles to perform the ceremony.

Steven asked me if I would officiate their wedding, and I told him I would be honored. He thanked me, and plans for their ceremony were made. When my new friends arrived at The Fountains for their wedding, the grounds were prepared. The pecan orchard would serve as a natural background for the ceremony. As I stood presiding over the first wedding at The Fountains, I told their friends and family that it was my pleasure to introduce Steven and Barbara as man and wife. For me, I felt as though I were introducing more than just my two friends; I was introducing my brother and sister in Christ.

My hurtful past that could have resulted in an attitude of bitterness helped me develop and exercise true love and forgiveness. I looked at Steven standing in the shadows of The Fountains, the house where he was raised, and then I turned slightly and looked at the cotton field, remembering the innocent little six-year-old boy who uttered the "N" word that could have forever shaken my life. Although the name he called us pierced my heart like a knife, I didn't allow that wound to stay with me. In fact, the pain and the scar healed as I grew in the Lord and understood His purpose for my life. I remember God teaching me an important principle: *When the pain of your past can be met with purpose, then your very existence can offer you clarity and meaning.*

It was revealed to me once I moved back to Arkansas, that God had assigned other people to come alongside me. Over time, I was blessed to realize that the ones who were assigned were some of the same people I had lived with in my past. There are people walking alongside my ministry today whom I met when I was a college student in 1975. I wish for the readers of this book to understand that the great blessing is that I am not serving in the ministry by myself, but I am happily working with people whom I have met along my way.

A NOTE FROM THE BOOK'S CO-AUTHOR
- Darrel Campbell

How does one measure a man's life? Specifically, how could one measure the life of Charles Graham? Is it the tangible things that he has accomplished, the plaques on the wall, his honorary doctorate, the photographs with heads of state, his famous relationships, or the number of music recordings made or sold? The miles traveled are now incalculable. His public accomplishments are many, but I am convinced that it is the innumerable points of contact Charles has encountered over six decades that make up the uniqueness of his life journey.

When I first met the interesting young man from Dermott, Arkansas, I had recently suffered the worst loss of my young life. Three weeks before Charles and I shook hands for the first time, I had stood at the foot of the grave of my best friend, who was tragically taken from me. A hollow feeling consumed me as I attempted to go on with life, acting as if nothing had changed. No one could take the place of the friend I had lost, of course. That's not how life works, I learned. My next discovery about life was how God could mend my broken heart by bringing new relationships to intersect my personal trek through life.

Charles Graham and I have been consistent friends for over forty years. In those decades there have been many parallel experiences and many hundreds more varied experiences as he pursued his dream and I pursued mine. Over those blessed years, I have observed a man whom God wanted me to know. He has often been the solid spiritual mortar between the bricks that make up so much of my life's structure. My best friend whom I lost just before I started college had been as close as any brother could be. Never would I have imagined that someone else could be as close.

For the longest time, I thought that my brother Charles Graham and I had a unique camaraderie. When my wife and I lived on the East Coast of the United States, he visited us. When my career called me to Hollywood, God called him west, and he bought a home not far from my wife and me in Los Angeles. Our friendship continued to grow in California. When I moved my family back to my childhood home in the Midwest, God called Charles back to his childhood home in the Deep South. Through all the moves the brotherhood remained, but it wasn't until later in our adulthood I realized that our friendship was not so unique. I discovered that the magnetism of Charles Graham has drawn hundreds of friends like me into his sphere of influence.

A simple example of how Charles treats his Christian family members can be found in a brief story that includes his assistant, Lori. It seems that one of Charles Graham's admirers, a sweet senior citizen woman, called the ministry one afternoon to leave Charles a message. At the end of the call, Lori asked if she could take the name of the gentle lady who was calling. Lori told the woman she would be happy to give Charles the message, and he would be happy to return the woman's call.

"Oh, you just tell him that Mom called," the lady told Lori.

"Mom, who?" Lori inquired.

"Oh, he will know. Just tell him Mom will be waiting for his call," she replied.

And with that confident remark, the elderly woman hung up the phone. Needless to say, when Charles received the message from his assistant to "call Mom," he had no idea which of his many Moms in the world wished to visit with him on the telephone. Thanks to "caller i.d." he was able to figure out which "Mom" had called.

As I have traveled across the country with Charles, it has become very clear that my brother has hundreds of friends who consider him to be one of their best friends. He has dozens of blood relatives, which include more nieces and nephews than I can recount. I am certain that his blood relatives have no clue of the thousands of persons in America, Europe, the Middle East, and Africa who believe they are just as personally close to him as any of his family members. I assure you that there are "Moms" and "Pops" in virtually every continent and country he has visited during his ministry.

Permit me to share just a few notes we received from around the world while writing *No Back Doors*.

In 2012, my husband went to be with the Lord, leaving a large vacancy in our family. His death also meant that the church we had pioneered and pastored for thirty-three years was without a pastor. The events and challenges that I faced in the days and months that followed rendered my heart fertile ground for unforgiveness and bitterness. At this very vulnerable time, The Lord sent Charles Graham to guide me on the journey of forgiveness and restoration. It was a road he had personally traveled, and his counsel was always based on the Word of God. He not only prayed for me, but he walked me through the process, reminding me of the Father's love, encouraging me to pray for my

*enemies, and teaching me to give to those who had
wounded me. I know of no other person who reflects the
character of our Father better than Charles. - Debbie*

*I spent an entire day with Charles in San Diego. I
felt as if he was a celebrity because everywhere we went
someone knew him or knew someone who knew him! I am
impressed by Charles' love for people. His catchphrase,
"You're a blessing," is always upbeat and sincere.
Charles has proved to be a faithful and true friend these
past twenty-five years. He is also a role model of a man
of God. I asked him to be the godfather of our son, Caleb
Graham (his namesake), and it is important to me to pass
down to my son the many blessings I received because I
have known Charles. I've watched him in a movie, I
attended his honorary doctorate ceremony, I attended his
fiftieth birthday party, as well as the dedication of The
Fountains. - Jody (and wife Dora)*

*Years ago we hosted four college students in our
home, and one of them was Charles Graham. Late one
night after church, the young men came to our home, and
we had already gone to bed. Curiosity got the best of
Charles, so he lifted the cover to our house's vacuum
system, and it roared through the house. Without the
attachments it sounded like an airplane taking off! Years
of visits followed, and Charles stayed with us often. Our
conversations at home with Charles have varied from
silly to serious, soul-searching and prayers, advice given
and advice taken. Once while Charles visited my
daughter at SMU, one of the coeds said, "Hey, I know
you! You're Jill's brother! I've seen your picture on her
bulletin board." During our vacation in Mexico, Charles*

met us there, and by the end of the week, people managing restaurants and shops were waving and shouting, "Carlos" to Charles as we passed by. When we first met Charles, he shared with us some of his personal story, but we could have never guessed how much God's blessings would pour down on Charles in the years ahead. The Lord has touched three generations through Charles. We consider Charles a son and a brother. Our seven grandchildren have known "Uncle Charles" since birth. - Mike and Carol

Charles and I debated whether or not to put people's names or quotations in this book simply because of all of his friends and family who would be omitted. He has lost track of the births he has witnessed, the weddings and funerals he has officiated and the graduations, anniversaries, dedications, award ceremonies, games, concerts, plays, and birthday parties he has attended around the world. Had we named them all, this book would have undoubtedly grown into a ten-volume set.

I share the previous three quotes with the readers of this book as evidence of how I discovered that the uniqueness of my friendship with Charles Graham isn't all that unique. I have learned that there are thousands of people across the world who say the same things about their relationship with Charles. What I have discovered is the uniqueness of the man. If the measure of Charles Graham's life is the number of people he has personally influenced during his ministry, then his life stretches thousands of miles wide and hundreds of miles high. It is risky to look at any human being as a role model, and Charles would be the first person to tell you that it is only the person of Jesus Christ in Charles that matters.

Our brother Charles has walked by faith and not by sight every year of his ministry. I have been with him when he had nothing in his pockets and when he wondered where the gas for his old van, "Nicodemus," was coming from. I have heard story after story of God showing up in the nick of time so Charles could keep his ministry going and at the same time help someone else who was struggling. I have prayed for him and beside him. He has prayed dozens of times for my family and me. When illness and loss struck our family, it was Charles we wanted nearby. We have laughed together and cried together. I've seen him give away his last dollar, and I have watched him as he collected school supplies so he could give them away for free to every single student in need. Charles wants no child in school to feel out of place, or to do without. I have seen him treat the very old and the very young with the greatest of respect, and I've heard him say to each in his genuine way, *You're a ... pause... blessing.* He usually makes the children say the word "blessing" before he does.

Although this book is hundreds of pages long and contains numerous personal stories, there are thousands more moments of connection you will never hear of because my brother Charles is also a private and humble man. To many of the readers of this book, Charles is a wonderful singer and minister. To others he is like a son. To thousands, he is a brother. To tens of thousands of children, including my own, he is simply "Uncle Charles."

When I hear people talk about the family of God, I think of how much better the world would be if all our family members were as kind and loving as Charles Graham. To all who have known Charles, he has given them a taste of what the great family reunion will be like in Heaven. There will be no humiliation or standing at the back door.

As in the life of Charles, waiting for us at the front door we will find honor, respect, dignity, worth, and unending love because God's love made a Way for us all.

- Darrel Campbell

EPILOGUE

In conclusion, I wanted to tell my story to make sure my message of hope transcends who I am. My place of new ministry was ironically waiting for me in the oldest place of familiarity— the place where it all started. The invigorating joy of life and living could only be experienced at a new level because of my choice to live back in Arkansas. Re-establishing myself in the rural fields of the South allowed me to see things this time around that I did not see the first time around. I now know that although I was living in a racially divided community during my youth, there were many wonderful people from my past who genuinely and sincerely cared about me. Sadly, during that time in our nation, many were unable to express the truth of their hearts. These days, I can sit for hours with people in my community and visit about the past. As we converse, I learn their stories, and I am amazed and blessed at this truth. Most of all, I want people to know the role my faith in God has played in my life story, for without faith there would be no such story, certainly not this one.

Now that you have read my story, please allow me to share one last thought. As I was writing this book and trying to decide what the title should be, my co-author and I concluded it should be, *No Back Doors*. When God allowed me to own the house where as a boy I had to stand at the back door to collect my pay, it was nothing short of a miracle. It was also the catalyst for writing the book. As my personal story began to unfold in the house, the physical back door of my home would often remind me of past hurts, pains, and disappointments. But, having lived in the house for nearly ten years now, God has moved me forward and beyond the backdoor's image and negative thoughts.

The title, *No Back Doors,* no longer serves as a reminder of the physical back door on the house, but rather a metaphor for the past hurts. I have been blessed to live in God's ability to move me beyond the "back doors" of my life. Although your back doors may not look like mine, it's safe to say that we all have back doors we need to move beyond.

My prayer for you is that when you finish this book you will allow the Holy Spirit to minister God's truth that He is able to move you beyond the back doors of your life. In the Bible, Paul wrote this verse to the Philippians: Not that I have already attained or have already been perfected, but I follow after it so that I may lay hold of that for which I was seized by Christ Jesus. Brothers, I do not count myself to have attained, but this one thing I do, forgetting those things which are behind and reaching forward to those things which are ahead, I press toward the goal to the prize of the high calling of God in Christ Jesus. (Philippians 3:12-14 MEV)

36024531R00155

Made in the USA
Middletown, DE
10 February 2019